C000318849

400

Spirit in the Stone

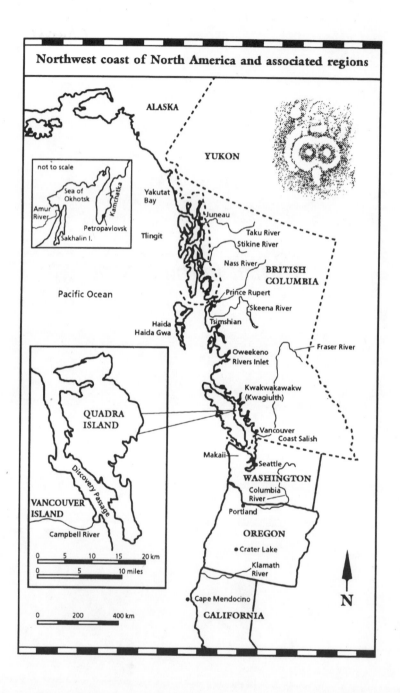

Northwest coast of North America and associated regions

ALASKA

YUKON

not to scale

Sea of Okhotsk

Kamchatka

Amur River

Petropavlovsk

Sakhalin I.

Yakutat Bay

Juneau

Taku River

Stikine River

Tlingit

Nass River

BRITISH COLUMBIA

Pacific Ocean

Prince Rupert

Skeena River

Haida
Haida Gwa

Tsimshian

Oweekeno
Rivers Inlet

Fraser River

Kwakwakawakw
(Kwagiulth)

QUADRA ISLAND

Vancouver

Coast Salish

Makaii

Seattle

Discovery Passage

WASHINGTON

VANCOUVER ISLAND

Columbia River

Campbell River

Portland

0   5   10   15   20 km

OREGON

0   5   10 miles

Crater Lake

Klamath River

Cape Mendocino

N

CALIFORNIA

0   200   400 km

Spirit in the Stone

Joy Inglis

HORSDAL & SCHUBART

Horsdal & Schubart Publishers Ltd.
Victoria, BC, Canada

Front-cover photograph by Rolf Bettner, Ottawa and Victoria.

All drawings of petroglyphs and pictographs by Hilary Stewart, Quadra Island, BC.

Maps by Kathy Curry, Vancouver, BC.

This book is set in Galliard.

We acknowledge the support of the Canada Council for the Arts for our publishing program.

Printed and bound in Canada by Printcrafters Inc., Winnipeg, Manitoba.

Canadian Cataloguing in Publication Data

Inglis, Joy, 1919-
  Spirit in the stone

Includes bibliographical references.
ISBN 0-920663-58-3

  1. Petroglyphs--British Columbia--Quadra Island. 2. Indians of North America--British Columbia--Quadra Island--Antiquities. 3. Indians of North America--British Columbia--Quadra Island--Antiquities--Religious aspects. 4. Quadra Island (B.C.)--Antiquities. I. Title.
E78.B9I53 1998   709'.01'130899707112   C98-910109-6

Printed and bound in Canada

To Beth

FOREWORD

In the lost arts, the lost ways, the stolen ways of my people, knowledgeable persons asked the Creator for energy to go into rock, into air, into water. They trained to become one with these elements. The White man came along and spoiled our vision. The Elders are buried who did these things. The truth can not come out because we are not on your path, Great Spirit.

Petroglyphs are gifts from the Creator who gave shamans sheer energy to go into the rock, their fingers hot with a power like electricity. It was not the body that could do all these things but the soul, the spirit; not the person but the other self, the extension of self. Some people in Japan train to break apart a plank with the edge of their hand. It was explained to me that the sheer energy breaks the board, while the hand carries the force through. That is the way with going into rock.

Rock carvings are all over the world. In New Zealand I learned that their rocks tell creation stories. Our rocks are evidence of the Creator's gifts. They are there to pass on this knowledge to anybody who studies them.

Ellen White
Kwulasulwut Elder, Nanaimo Band
writer, and Elder-in-Residence of First Nations program,
Malaspina College, Nanaimo, B.C.

CONTENTS

Acknowledgments

I have dedicated this book to Beth Hill. It owes a great deal to Beth and Ray's initial research and publication, and to Beth's enthusiasm for the publication of this book. Beth's posthumous work, *Moonrakers*, reveals a life of startling personal visionary experiences at rock-art sites on the North Pacific Coast and in Europe. She worked with professional psychics as one means by which scientific observation could be supplemented by some techniques of vision used by the rock artists themselves. Appendix One of this book gives a recollection of one such reading by Dyan Grant-Francis of Victoria, who accompanied Beth at her request to the "Shamans' Pool" at Kulleet Bay near Ladysmith. Also AlixSandra Parness, a well-known clairvoyant energy healer from the United States, visited Quadra Island in 1996 and gives us, in Appendix Two, her reading of two outstanding petroglyphs here, the "Seawolf" and "The Lovers." Thank you, Sandi.

Heartfelt thanks to Marcy Wolter, my exploring companion and research enthusiast over the years. She has felt an awe in the presence of the petroglyphs, and sensed the spirit in the stone. Many of the petroglyphs shown in the book were located by Marcy, who is an expert at sensing significant clues that indicate where petroglyphs may be found, and identifying them. At this time of my life, when I can no longer walk surefooted over the trails and scramble over driftwood and rock to reach the sites, Marcy continues the research.

I am profoundly grateful to my friend and colleague Hilary Stewart, who encouraged me to turn a proposed pamphlet into a book, and produced over 60 original pen-and-ink drawings to illustrate and embellish the text.

Ross Henry, assisted by Janice Kenyon, provided a photographic record of the petroglyphs in their natural settings. Special thanks for their night-light photography that proved so important in the quest for new finds, and in the discovery of previously unnoticed detail on known rock carvings.

Julie Campbell, author and photographer, caught the "spirit in the stone" in dawn and dusk photographs of elusive petroglyphs. Geologist Malcolm Campbell has examined and identified the petroglyph rocks at all sites.

David Smith and Nancy Allwarden visited all sites by boat or hiking trail, and measured the relevant boulders, the relationship between them, and their orientation to nearby streams and other features. They produced the information for the maps in Part Two to show routes of access to the public beaches where petroglyphs are located. For their many hours of work on the project, I am deeply appreciative.

Thank you to Kathy Curry of Vancouver, for drawing the final maps for the book.

Thanks to distinguished artists Susan Point, Dempsey Bob, Bill Reid, Roy Vickers, Greg Colfax, Bob Cranmer, Pam Holloway, Mark Henderson and Dora Sewid Cook for permission to reproduce their work in this book. I am grateful to Roy Vickers, one of the masters of contemporary Northwest Coast art, who has permitted the reproduction of the crest which honours his mother's clan.

Thank you, Judy Williams, for a painter's assessment of the petroglyph carving at Forward Harbour. So many elements associated with petroglyphs of the Northwest Coast in their settings were highlighted in your first-person account.

I gratefully acknowledge the assistance of the Kwagiulth Museum and Cultural Centre at Cape Mudge, Quadra Island, where for many years I have conducted field trips to petroglyph sites for staff and visitors and have given lectures sponsored by the museum. The enthusiasm and cooperation of staff member Gerrie Dinsley, who arranges rock-art programs in the museum, has been important to sustaining the energy of the on-going project which resulted in this book. Thank you to Barry Calverley, Wendy Terrell, Jim Leishman, Bob Sivertson, Anita Stewart, Gerry Dick and other Quadra Islanders who recently found unrecorded petroglyphs and led us to their locations.

This book has been many years in the writing. From the beginning, I consulted with archaeologists Roy Carlson and Doris Lundy. Doris read an early draft of the manuscript. Neither they nor any other professionals I consulted are responsible for errors on my part. Thanks to my husband, Bob, whose never-failing belief in me and my works lasted through our lives together and even into these declining years when his love and encouragement sustain me still. Thank you, son Stephen Inglis and daughter-in-law Erica Claus, for suggestions and ideas for presentation. Thank you, Paulette and Len, for assistance with manuscript review. I owe a great deal to my nephew, Clare Caldicott, who, in his ardent zeal for the publication of this work, bought me a computer, taught me to use it, and backed me up with sustained practical and moral support throughout the years of discovery and writing. He did this while commuting between his home in Victoria and our home on Quadra Island, some hundred miles apart, to answer my calls for help. Before we concluded this work, he deserted me for Australia. Luckily my neighbour, Chris Thompson, became the technical expert who rescued me from on-going computer disaster. He reviewed my final draft for this book with his usual devotion, wisdom, and unruffled serenity. Thank you, Chris.

An early grant from the Regional District of Campbell River encouraged the research and writing of *Spirit in the Stone*.

Joy Inglis, Quadra Island, B.C., December 1997

EXPLORING THE ROCK-ART TRADITION OF THE NORTHWEST COAST

This book is about rock carvings of the coastal areas of northwest America, a part of the world where from the earliest times of settlement by First Nations peoples even the simplest tools were embellished with carvings. From indigenous societies where every man was a carver, distinguished artists developed, working within a recognized tradition that was expressed in individual styles of the various groups along the coast. The unifying element in all Northwest Coast art is making the spirits of the unseen world visible. This applies to petroglyph art as well. The symbols carved upon rock are the shamans' spirits. This is the "spirit in the stone."

Information for this book was sought from native respondents, from archaeologists, from published sources, and from psychics who make use of some of the shamanic techniques of the carvers of the petroglyphs. Most of what I learned came from exploring the beaches of Quadra Island for rock art, and learning from the petroglyphs themselves what is the key to their nature and distribution, and where they are likely be found.

John Moon of the native village of Cape Mudge first showed our family the symbols carved on rocks at the Tsa-Kwa-Luten site on Quadra Island in 1963. I found them powerfully intriguing. It is a fascination that has persisted through the passing years.

A deeper appreciation of petroglyphs comes from long familiarity with each site. These insights have not figured in previous surveys of rock art along the coast, where the geographical scope of the inquiry is enormous, and the emphasis is on recording the carved symbols themselves. Those of us who worked to gather material for this book felt privileged to linger in the many places of wonder where petroglyphs are found. They should be respected and protected. Native people have described the petroglyph rocks as objects of veneration.

The importance of rock art to all humankind is increasingly acknowledged, now that it is recognized as a tradition common to all peoples (including Europeans) at a time when hunting and gathering characterized the mode of production.

On this coast, settlers had little interest in petroglyphs at a time when they were still being made or still in use. Native settlements and petroglyph sites on the Northwest Coast were, at the early years of contact, remote from the new towns. Those few clerics and teachers with a religious mission to live amongst the people regarded the work of the shaman as the work of the devil. In any case, training by shamans for the acquisition of powers from the spirit world was undertaken in secret places recognized as having supernatural potency. Some petroglyph sites are places where shamans trained youths for spirit power at puberty. I have relied on my own anthropological studies of the world view of aboriginal peoples in the Northwest Coast culture area for my interpretation of the shamanic belief system expressed in petroglyph art.

Societies along the Northwest Coast developed arts and ceremony to a degree unusual amongst hunting and gathering populations. Theirs was a highly organized society. Their winter villages have existed on the same site for thousands of years. Vast annual runs of salmon were harvested in the same way agriculturists are dependent on their annual harvest of crops. The development of their arts and rich spiritual life was in part due to the abundance and seasonal nature of their food supply.

Research by archaeologists into the nature of petroglyphs scattered over the thousands of miles of the Northwest Coast and up rivers in this enormous territory is providing new perspectives in the once-obscure field of petroglyph art. Some of the symbols carved in the rocks, such as humans, birds and other animals, can be reliably identified, and related to myths. Their precise age or purpose is still a matter for conjecture. Cumulative on-going laboratory research into images produced in deliberately altered states of consciousness may help to explain some of the features of symbols such as auras and spirals.

Many petroglyphs are located near the salmon-spawning streams owned by lineages in coastal aboriginal societies. The economy of the Northwest Coast peoples was based on a wide variation in the nature and availability of the food resources, the greatest resource being fish. Quadra Island in the Strait of Georgia, where the petroglyphs discussed in Part Two of this book are located, is a renowned fishing area. In 1971, Don Mitchell, archaeologist at the University of Victoria, and the leading authority on this region, described it in this way: "The Gulf of Georgia is set off from regions to the south, and from all other neighboring regions by the magnitude and quality of the fish runs passing through the Gulf and entering the Fraser River."[1]

The pre-contact population, now known to have been much greater than earlier suspected, was dependent upon the seasonal runs of salmon whose return could not be left to chance, but required the powerful supernatural magic for which shamans trained. Native people feel that being a fishing people defines them. "Fishing is our living, our way of life."[2]

I was joined early in this research by my friend and fellow-researcher Marcy Wolters and the ideas expressed in this book come from our shared experience.

The richness of Quadra Island rock art only became evident with our increasing familiarity with the petroglyph figures known to us in the 1960s. Working with the staff of the Kwagiulth Museum and Cultural Centre at Cape Mudge, we found, by close observation and by running our hands across the rocks, many details of body parts and head gear overlooked on familiar images of faces. More and more astonishing petroglyphs were discovered at many more sites. It was time to record findings and express what we had learned about the rock carvings.

Part One of the book is comprised of field-work observation, insights gained by my association with Ellen White (a spirit dancer and healer of the Nanaimo people), and knowledge gained from many years of work and friendship with First Nations people at the village of Cape Mudge as a named and adopted participant in their work and ceremonies. Studies in anthropology at the University of British Columbia gave me the necessary background in ethnology. Six years of discussions with Harry Assu, an Elder at Cape Mudge village, in preparation for the publication of his memoirs, deepened my understanding of two worlds of thought.

At one time I had thought of petroglyph art as being of a separate and often bizarre nature, outside the mainstream of the coastal carvers' art in wood. Howard White, upon seeing the famous petroglyph, "The Deer's Head," at Robber's Nob near Port Neville, wrote that most petroglyphs he'd seen "showed no more sense of artistic form than a bunch of graffiti on a warehouse wall, obviously not done by the same hands that made the highly formalized designs on the house fronts and totem poles."[3]

By chance, I saw for myself that petroglyph form and meaning are an integral part of the great tradition of Northwest Coast art. While speaking to the public on the lower floor of the Kwagiulth Museum at Cape Mudge, I realized that the Quadra Island petroglyphs in the slides and rubbings being shown had their parallels in the wood carvings on display in the main gallery upstairs. On exhibition was the museum's "Potlatch Collection" of 19th- and 20th-century masks and regalia taken away by agents of the federal government and police from the local Lekwiltok (Kwagiulth) Bands in 1922. In the carvings on boulders placed outside the museum and in situ on the beaches of Quadra Island, and in the masks of wood in the museum's collection, there is the same emphasis on numerous spirit heads of human proportions, some with various elaborations of fins, teeth, and beaks that indicate another species, or express the duality of humans and other animals by the representations of multiple beings in one body.

It should be borne in mind that the forceful and intriguing petroglyphs from Quadra Island indicate the range of production of only one type of work in stone, and on only one island, whether "artistic" in our terms or not, while the photographs in this book of 19th-century carvings in museums, and the art of living masters to which petroglyph art is compared, are examples of pieces selected by connoisseurs of western art, from the vast range of art products of the extensive Northwest Coast area.

Today, the art of coastal masters, working in the same tradition, has entered the mainstream of the international art market, so that the artist is always known and acknowledged, and accepts commissions not only from persons in his own community of origin for authentic traditional events, but also from patrons and institutions worldwide.

I have not made comparisons in terms of artistic merit as judged by those outside the native culture. Works from various periods are compared only in terms of structure and style, and most important, in what I have come to feel constitutes a palpable connection to the supernatural that is difficult to express in words, but can be felt by the observer. It involves the viewer in the charge of energy generated by the artist and experienced by the artist as supernatural power.

Certain works by contemporary artists seem to capture this same magic of the spirit in the stone. Many agreed to having their work shown in this context in Part One, "The Tradition," and I acknowledge their generous contributions.

Native people on Quadra Island refer to themselves and their institutions as "Kwagiulth." I have followed their wishes in this respect.

They are the We-Wai-Kai Band, Lekwiltok-language speakers, and the southernmost band of the Kwagiulth Nation. The term "Kwakwaka 'wakw" (for speakers of the Kwakwala language), instituted by the U'Mista Society at Alert Bay, is not in general use here.

Rubbings with wax on cloth are permitted for research purposes but are otherwise discouraged at all sites by the Archaeological Branch of the provincial government which has responsibility for protection of archaeological sites. Taking rubbings of petroglyphs has no effect upon the stone images locally, where the rock is granite; it may however encourage defacement by vandals by other means.

There is a difference of opinion as to the best method of protection for rock-art sites in British Columbia. Some archaeologists hold that only professionals working within the provisions of the Archaeological Sites Protection Act should know their whereabouts, the location to be kept secret from the public. Since only a small handful of this select group has taken the time to visit the sites, our heritage is slowly eroding away without our knowledge.

The We-Wai-Kai Band, and the Kwagiulth Museum and Cultural Centre on Quadra Island have encouraged on-going research and publication. First Nations are very clear on their ownership of archaeological features such as petroglyphs. The Galgalis Project of the Kwakiutl Territorial Fisheries Commission, which represents Kwakwala, Leqwala and Comox speakers, is mapping specific sites in what was once their traditional territory, so that development and residential settlement that is going on apace in this territory will not destroy First Nations cultural and resource areas. The location and description of petroglyph sites and other heritage sites in the Kwakiutl Land and Sea Claims Territory will provide information upon which decisions on protection can be based. I hope this book will contribute to that knowledge.

PART ONE

THE STONE

Petroglyphs (Greek: *petra,* rock; *glyph*, carving) are signs and symbols of spiritual significance, pitted and grooved into rock. They are found in widely separated areas on nearly all the continents of the world, a record left by hunting and gathering societies that stretches back from this century into antiquity. On the North Pacific coast, petroglyphs are carved into rock boulders and rock faces from Siberia through Alaska to northern California. They are also found inland, often on the salmon-spawning rivers of this immense region: the Amur, Stikine, Skeena, Bella Coola, Fraser and Columbia.

The frontispiece map shows the Northwest Coast Culture Area, a convenient ethnographic designation for a group of rainforest societies sharing many features of a common culture. It is this region the book focuses upon. The area extends from Yakutat Bay in southeastern Alaska to Cape Mendocino in northern California. The distance is more than 2,300 km as the raven flies. The actual coastline distance is vastly greater, especially in the northern regions, with deep fjords and a rugged coastline. What distinguishes this region is the reliance of the native people on salmon. Their way of life was

1

based on fishing, preserving and storing salmon, and it is to this vital trait that we can look for associated meanings of their ancient petroglyph tradition.

"The Orator," petroglyph at Tsa-Kwa-Luten, L3, Quadra Island.

a) Distinction between Pictographs and Petroglyphs

It is customary to make a distinction between different kinds of rock art: pictographs and petroglyphs. Pictographs are paintings, usually in black, or in red ochre, a pigment ground from certain rocks. These pictures occur along rock ledges by the sea, and along lakes, up rivers and on valley trails in the Interior of B.C. Petroglyphs are carvings. A few instances of painted petroglyphs have been recorded by native people and are mentioned below. No paint is discernible now on petroglyphs.

More petroglyphs have been found along the coast than in the Interior. They are likely to be found at the mouths of salmon-spawning streams where the First Peoples established their villages. Frequently, they are located in the river canyons at prime fishing stations. Doris Lundy has pointed out that of the 16 petroglyph sites

2

Pictograph in red paint, Christina Lake. (FROM CORNER, *PICTOGRAPHS*)

found in the Interior, most are along the middle Fraser River and the major motive behind their creation relates to the salmon resource.

According to Annie York, the subject matter of pictographs in the Stein River Valley is stories, legends and dreams. The play of the brush or stick allowed the painter a looser and livelier depiction than is the case with carving stone, where the images must be beaten into lines of pits and then grooved. The heavy work in stone is reflected in the ponderous and sombre nature of petroglyph figures. Petroglyphs are the consequence of shamanic rituals intended to bring in the runs of fish and thus ensure the survival of the people.

Ellen White, Kwulasulwut Elder, Nanaimo Band, spirit dancer and healer, makes a distinction between "picture paints" and "rock carvings": "They [petroglyphs] can keep the ways of these people alive, not only here but it seems all over the world. We definitely feel the energies, the shock waves."[1]

The term "writing on rock" has been used to comprise both traditions of psychic visualization and inscription, whether painted or carved. Annie York, however, considered pictographs and petroglyphs to be the same phenomenon. Annie explained that a carved boulder with typical petroglyph designs upon it, found in the Fraser River in 'Nlaka'pamux territory, was painted after it was carved. "It started out they scraaaaaach and then they fill it with paint. Same as that one up here in the hills above Chapman's [the McDonald petroglyphs]. Chief Henry James says that those things are painted in the first place, but he says so long that the rain hits them and they got washed out."[2] As to purpose, Annie said, "You have to ask God to help you, that you gonna use this drawing in later life — that's going to be your strength too."[3]

Anthropologist Homer Barnett was informed by his native respondent Albert Westley that the Jack Point petroglyph at the estuary of the Nanaimo River was painted when the salmon ran poorly or late. According to the late Sam Henderson, singer and carver from Campbell River, born in Blunden Harbour, the petroglyphs at Cape Mudge on Quadra Island were said to be painted red on occasion to warn the Blunden Harbour people that the dreaded Haida were ahead at the present village of Cape Mudge.

There are no painted petroglyphs in B.C. now. Only the pictographs retain their paint.

b) Dating Petroglyphs

The earliest piece of art, a whalebone pendant resembling a rockfish, comes from the site of Namu, B. C., dating to about 3,500 years ago. It is difficult to know with certainty when the petroglyphs were first made in North America. Archaeological evidence suggests that the time of arrival of early hunting and fishing populations on the Northwest Coast may be as early as 13,000 to 12,000 years ago, and the route was by way of a land bridge over what is now the Bering Strait. This theory is objected to by aboriginal people today whose origin stories tell of the creation of the clans in their current territories. In either case, there is no evidence of human occupation on the

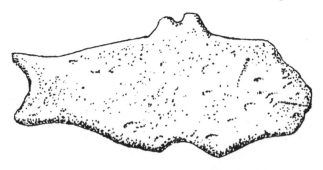

Whalebone pendant resembling a rockfish, from a site at Namu.
(FROM CARLSON, *INDIAN ART TRADITIONS*)

Northwest Coast before 10,000 ago. The oldest sites on the coast known to archaeology are dated from 9,700 years ago at Namu on the central coast, and from 9,000 years ago at sites on the Fraser River.

Another pendant, made from antler, with figures back to back comes from Kwantna on the central coast and dates to 1400 to 1800 A.D. Roy Carlson, archaeologist at Simon Fraser University, asks, "Are they twins, widespread in North American mythology and here associated with the salmon?"[4]

Antler pendant, actual size. Figures back to back.
(FROM CARLSON, *INDIAN ART TRADITIONS*)

Doris Lundy, archaeologist and rock-art specialist, theorizes that the "tradition" of making petroglyphs was brought across to North America from Siberia with the First Peoples. "The actual petroglyphs made could not last more than 3,000 years on the gale-swept beaches of this region. Perhaps a few in extremely sheltered situations might escape erosion over time, and still be seen today. The difficulty is determining which of the petroglyphs are older. Unless they are buried in such a way as to suggest their age by the dating of associated materials at that depth, there is no way of dating these exposed rocks with petroglyphs incised on them."[5] According to

Lundy it is a logical possibility that petroglyphs on this coast are from 300 to 3,000 years old.

While petroglyphs worldwide differ in style and content consistent with the culture that produced them, they frequently share certain configurations associated with induced hallucination and altered states of consciousness, such as spirals, heads with auras, and other elements of psychic vision. Petroglyphs from the lower basin of the Amur River in Siberia, dated to the third millennium B.C., show a similarity to the most basic, ancient and widespread style of rock carving on the Northwest Coast — enough to suggest a possible common ancestry. For example, simple and forceful relief drawings on rock of the underwater monster, Master of the Amur, as well as drawings of birds, skulls and animals are basically in a style that is common to the Northwest Coast.

Some similarities with the Amur petroglyphs are seen on Quadra Island in the "radiant masks" and skull-shaped heads, and in the X-ray art, where the ribs and inner body parts of an animal are depicted within an outline of the form.

According to Roy Carlson, evidence for art in archaeological sites is late in the prehistoric record — around 2,500 years ago. It

Rayed-head petroglyph, Kwagiulth Museum, L2.

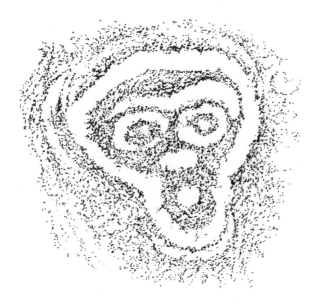

Skull-like petroglyph, Kwagiulth Museum, L2.

was at that time that techniques were developed for incising and pecking stone to make small portable artifacts, in the same style as petroglyphs. The important developmental period for Northwest Coast art styles was from 2,500 to 1,500 years ago. Small sculptures of naturalistic animal figures, especially birds from this period, show a startling continuity with the style of birds on petroglyphs seen today.

So far as dating petroglyph art is concerned, Carlson says that an important impetus for producing carvings is evident about 1,500

Bird form incised and sculptured in antler. Buckle. 1100 B.C.- A.D. 350.
(FROM CARLSON, *INDIAN ART TRADITIONS*)

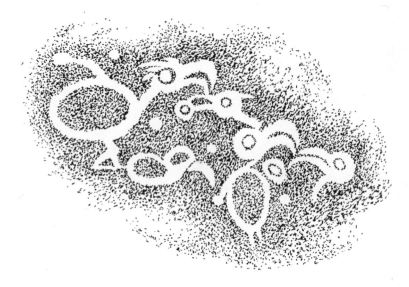

Panel of birds, Tsa-Kwa-Luten, L3.

years ago, a period of flowering in the arts, when a shift occurred in society from art in a religious context to art which could serve the growing need of families for status symbols. Indications of this change of focus come from sites at Namu, Prince Rupert harbour, and Musqueam, where various elements, such as differentiation in amounts of grave goods, head deformation associated with status, lip ornaments of high-ranking persons, and sophisticated art suggest full-time artists and commissioned art. Evidently a culture based on the prestige and rank of extended families provided a stimulus for art, including petroglyph art.

On the world stage, the oldest agreed date for rock art is 32,000 years ago, in the caves of Chauvet and Cosquer in France where the old, finely worked panels are still in a good state of preservation.

A storm of skepticism from rock-art specialists has broken over a claim of twice that age for rock carvings discovered by Richard Fullegar and his associates at Jinmium on the Kimberly Plateau in Western Australia. A slab of rock with characteristic pits, which must have sheared off from the rock face above and been buried under sediment, was dated to at least 58,000 years ago, a time before modern humans were thought to have entered Australia from the east.

Thomas Dowson, a research fellow at Southampton University, England, and a specialist on rock art, said in connection with the Australian claims, "Dating rock art is probably one of the most difficult things to do. I don't believe there has ever been a date produced that is not in some way contentious. A date of 40,000 years has been placed on rock art in Brazil, which no one will accept."[6]

This rejection out of hand of such an early date for rock art in the Americas is not necessarily accepted by the archaeological community working on this continent. Many believe that humankind could have left Asia in two different ice-age phases prior to the last formation of a land bridge over the Bering Strait, one of these being around 40,000 years ago. It is only the hard evidence required for dating the rock art that is in question, and many Americanists have accepted a date of 40,000 years for Brazil. Any date around 10,000 years for rock art seems to be assured of worldwide acceptance, given confirmation by modern dating techniques.

The oldest dated rock art in the Pacific Northwest is a deeply carved petroglyph panel which was found partly buried by ash from the explosion of Mount Mazama, which formed Oregon's Crater Lake some 6,700 years ago. Anthropologist Robert Heizer suggests that the native people were probably making petroglyphs before this date.

The only accurately dated petroglyph in British Columbia was reported by researcher Ann McMurdo, on Protection Island, near Nanaimo. Two radio-carbon dates were obtained from charcoal in stratified midden material partly overlying the petroglyph image of a killer whale, roughly pecked into sandstone, which forms the upper portion of a seaward bank. A young boy discovered the petroglyph when he accidentally removed some midden soil covering it, while swinging on a nearby maple tree.

A dig was conducted at this site in the 1970s. McMurdo stated in her report of the excavation that a date of approximately 345 years (plus or minus 40 years), was secured by radio-carbon dating, and is probably accurate, since the sample was obtained from a deep layer in the dig, less subject to modern contamination.

A pregnant whale petroglyph is carved on a beach boulder about a mile and a half south of Ozette, an archaeological village site on the western shore of the Olympic Peninsula. The image depicted on the rock closely resembles the outline of a whale incised on interior house boards in a great whaler's house at Ozette. A mud slide generally thought to have occurred some 500 years ago collapsed the houses in

Whale figure, Ozette, Washington. (FROM A PHOTOGRAPH BY RUTH KIRK, *EXPLORING WASHINGTON ARCHAEOLOGY*)

such a way that the contents were preserved and are on exhibition in a museum at Neah Bay.

Because of the close association of outline and general conception of the whale on the petroglyph with the whale on the house planks, the petroglyph is likely to date to the same time period. The carving of a pregnant whale suggests fecundity and the calling in of the greatest wealth conceivable for this whaling society.

Petroglyphs in the shape of "coppers" (symbols of wealth) are found inscribed on rocks at intervals along the Northwest Coast as far south as the north end of Vancouver Island. They date to the era of sailing ships when annealed copper sheets were carried on board for mending holes torn in the hull. The copper sheets were sought after as trade items by the native people who turned them into shield-shaped plaques, possibly used at first as body armour. Subsequently they became a symbol of wealth which could be displayed as grave markers, carved on memorial poles, as well as on boulders.

The actual coppers were bought and sold at ever increasing cost. Coppers have names, histories of purchase, and immense prestige value.

They are still exchanged today as bride-wealth, and bought and sold by their owners, or joint owners, for many thousands of dollars. While the original wealth represented was in valuables such as furs, slaves, oil, houses and canoes, it must be remembered that wealth ultimately rested upon access to and control of the salmon supply. In Kwagiulth territory, it has been shown that even the relative rank of villages themselves was based on their location with respect to the salmon.

Petroglyph in the shape of a copper. (FROM AN ILLUSTRATION BY B. AND R. HILL, *INDIAN PETROGLYPHS*)

Petroglyphs showing sailing ships are grooved on stone at Clo-oose, on the southwestern shore of Vancouver Island. These are post-contact carvings that hint at the power of calling in the wealth of the sea, in this case the cargo of trading ships.

Another instance of rock carving created after European contact is on the Englishman River on Vancouver Island where the petroglyph of a bear is carved on the sloping rock bluff above a gorge. Salmon were dip-netted there in the deep green pool below. Beth Hill wrote, "An elderly man now living there reports that his father worked on the construction across the river [at that point] in 1886, and at that time the deaf-mute Indian who had carved the pictures was among the Indians fishing there."[7]

Sailing ship carved in rock at Clo-oose, Vancouver Island.
(FROM AN ILLUSTRATION BY B. AND R. HILL, *INDIAN PETROGLYPHS*)

Bear petroglyph, Englishman River. (FROM AN ILLUSTRATION
BY B. AND R. HILL, *INDIAN PETROGLYPHS*)

12

THE INSPIRATION

What inspired the carvers to create images on rocks? Petroglyph art has been something of a mystery, often even to native people living near well-known sites. In a paper entitled "Petroglyphs in Southeastern Alaska," published in 1908, George T. Emmons wrote, "The present generation, even the oldest natives, have no knowledge of their origin or of their raison d'etre."[8]

In a similar vein, Edward Keithahn, working with the Tlingit of southeastern Alaska as Indian Affairs officer during the years 1929 to 1939, questioned old men who denied any knowledge of the meaning of petroglyphs or even that their people made them. One Haida informant did say they were made to cause rain. That seemed reasonable to Keithahn since salmon require fall rains in order to ascend the rivers to spawn, and the petroglyphs were most abundant on the beaches in front of the largest salmon-spawning streams, particularly sockeye salmon streams. While such early reports do not answer the question of why petroglyphs exist, Keithahn's report suggests a link to the salmon supply.

Some time after the establishment of Fort Rupert on Vancouver Island in 1850, a head was carved, amid a myriad of older petroglyph figures on a ledge of shelving sandstone rock at the beach, during the course of a Hamatsa Society drama in which a slave was seen to be shot on the beach. The head represented the Cannibal Monster, a figure who held the wild Hamatsa Society initiate in his thrall. The Hamatsa ritual did not become part of Kwagiulth ceremonies at Fort Rupert until the mid-19th century. The various phases of the Baxbaxw lanusiwe (Cannibal Monster) cycle of myth and ritual were introduced piecemeal through a number of marriages with the Rivers Inlet tribe. While it is possible to date one fairly recent petroglyph carving at Fort Rupert from this record, it does not help in dating the numerous other petroglyphs carved there prior to the singular event described above. Franz Boas reported in 1897 that "the Kwakiutl knew nothing of the events that ancient petroglyphs may have commemorated, but only that they were made at the time before animals were transformed into men."[9]

The Bella Coola, according to early reports, made petroglyphs in connection with the winter ceremonials of a secret society (likely the Hamatsa Society) and in this connection they drummed upon the rocks. This is one part of the puzzle of why pits are found on so many petroglyph rocks. (See The Mystery of the Pitted Rocks.)

Ritual at the splendid petroglyph originally on the Nanaimo River (now at the Nanaimo District Museum) was recalled by a native respondent in the 1950s: "One family in the nearby village of Salaxal possessed the knowledge (*siwin*) to induce the salmon to come."[10] On the Nanaimo River it was the fall run of chum salmon that were induced to come in, and for which certain First Salmon rites were anticipated. "When the salmon was late, the ritualist painted over these figures with red ochre; at the same time he also painted bits of four different substances, including goat wool and a grass, and burned them at the foot of the rock."[11] The ceremony at the petroglyph rock was remembered after white settlement but there is no way of knowing when this petroglyph was carved.

Though elements of petroglyph art are generally free-floating images, not organized into pictures that tell a story, our familiarity with European styles of painting inclines us to see in this extraordinary carving a tableau depicting salmon spirits swimming up the estuary of the Nanaimo River, the ripples gouged in stone. At right, below the water, what appears to be a fisher (an animal with potent

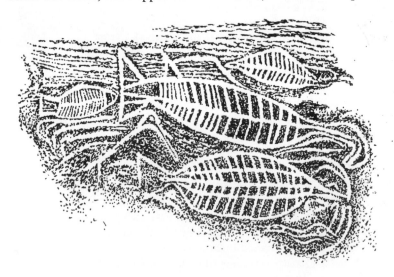

Petroglyph from Jack Point, Nanaimo Harbour.
(FROM A RUBBING BY BRUCE FINDLAYSON)

14

power for the shaman in Salish faith) leads the salmon upstream while a large, heron-like bird stands on the river bank looking into the scene. These salmon are represented life-like, with fins and tail, yet they are shown split and incised for wind and sun drying, just as they would be prior to being smoked to be used as part of the winter food supply.

Native people have given evidence at one time or another in the past about the reasons for making petroglyphs. These range from whiling away time waiting for the tide to change, to marking sacred space. Greg Colfax, tribal artist of Neah Bay, Washington, explains why petroglyphs were made: "They highlight places of power."[12] The most consistent explanation of why petroglyphs were made relates them to the sea, pools, rain and rivers, frequently salmon-spawning rivers.

On the Northwest Coast, petroglyphs are found at awe- inspiring locations, where spirit power was experienced, and still is experienced by some. (See appendices for reports by psychics Dyan Grant-Francis and AlixSandra Parness.) Petroglyphs are found primarily at salmon-spawning streams where the people lived, and at fishing stations on the upper reaches of rivers. These petroglyph sites, where shamans left the evidence of their powers in spirit figures carved on rock, became places of avoidance according to native respondents. Ritual training for supernatural power at puberty may have taken place there, as well as at more remote places. Some sites were very likely used by shamans when they gathered to demonstrate their powers. Ed Meade, first director of the Campbell River Museum and first to write on the petroglyphs of Quadra Island, was of the opinion that L3, the Tsa-Kwa-Luten site, was a place of power used by shamans for training initiates.

One secret location on nearby Cortes Island, while not a petro-glyph site, gives evidence of such a training site: "Xexgilh, 'Indian Doctors [shamans]' at Hurtado Point on Cortes Island has this name because it is believed that two double-headed serpents who were both Indian doctors lived in the two caves on this point.... People who wanted to have the double-headed serpent for their guardian spirit power would go to these caves...."[13] Shamans were known to dare to seek healing power from the double-headed sea serpent to add to the many spirit powers which they controlled.

The connection to the fish runs and salmon ceremony is a strong direct one, with much circumstantial evidence as well.

SPIRIT IN THE STONE

THE SPIRIT

a) The Dynamics of Transformation in Shamanic Art

It helps in decoding some glyphs with their cultural associations if something is known of the beliefs of the people who made them. The ideology that inspired the carvings is deeply rooted in the human psyche. One important aspect of shamanic ideology that is powerfully expressed amongst the peoples of this coast in mythology, ritual and art is the transformational nature of the world which begins in the creation story.

For the people of the Pacific Northwest, the creation of the world and the creation of humans took place long ago in myth time. A creative Trickster/ Transformer formed stones, mountains, islands and rivers from living beings. People were changed into birds, fish, mammals and rocks, and vice-versa, until the world took on its present appearance.

The Trickster/Transformer played many tricks in the process of creating the world. These became the basis of humorous tales told by the people, and of subtle surprises, puns and innuendoes in the arts. It would seem that the great creative Spirit of the people of the Northwest Coast was made in the image of sly humans, for this Being, especially on the central and northern coast and inland on the Plateau, was sexy, cunning, amusing and greedy in his tricky manoeuvres to create humans, bring light, and teach healing and practical skills.

In different societies along the coast this Transformer was experienced as disembodied power, or as a supernatural being in human form, or as a bird spirit like Raven or Crow. Raven was the great creator among the northern First Peoples in parts of Siberia, Alaska, the Queen Charlotte Islands and the Skeena River area. Farther down the coast, amongst the central and southern coastal peoples of British Columbia, this spirit took human form. He set things right and changed the appearance of all beings. Coyote was the Trickster/Creator on the mainland Plateau and in southern regions of the Northwest Coast. In 1963, Jim Naknakim, an Elder at Cape Mudge village on Quadra Island, told of the Transformer and how, when he came paddling down the coast, he spied village women hunched over on the beach digging clams. They were wearing cedar-bark capes and he changed them into river otters.

16

In coastal native cosmology, all things have a dual essence. All that was apparent took outward form in the far distant past at a time of transformation of the world. When the great power passed over the land and sea, changing the outward appearances of all forms of life, they became endowed with dual nature. Their present forms contain the essence of their original identities.

Rose Mitchell of Squirrel Cove on Cortes Island told a story about how Whale was transformed into Big Rock, a landmark boulder on a beach south of Campbell River.

"Mink was fishing near Mitlenatch Island when a big whale surfaced near him. Mink began making fun of Whale and bothered him so much that finally Whale swallowed both Mink and his canoe! Mink found himself in Whale's huge stomach surrounded by herring that Whale had swallowed. So Mink started a fire to cook some of these herrings, but he kept bumping his head against Whale's heart. Mink took his knife and sliced right through the heart, which caused Whale to beach himself. Some children who were playing nearby on the beach quickly ran to tell their parents about the whale. Soon people arrived ready to carve up the beached whale. Suddenly a voice was heard from inside the whale. It was Mink! The people cut through Whale's huge stomach and out jumped Mink. The heat from the fire had caused him to become bald. That whale is known today as Big Rock which is situated on the beach near Willow Point, just south of Campbell River."[14]

In his memoirs, Harry Assu, a distinguished Elder at Cape Mudge village, told a story about the human aspect of whales, and about people on the beach at Whisky Point on Quadra Island who resisted the Transformer and were turned into big boulders shaped like men.

In creation tales, animals, plants and rocks were changed into human form. Other living things, both plant and animal, and inanimate objects, such as islands, were created from humans. In all non-human forms, apparently inanimate such as boulders, the original pre-transformation form lies dormant. This is the unseen spirit in the stone. In visions of supernatural beings such as Bear, Wolf, Eagle, Whale or Sisiutl (sea serpent), sought out by youths on the spirit quest at puberty and by shamans, the human side was revealed to one purified by reason of ritual and self-denial into a state of bodily and spiritual clarity. The forms of life were changed, yet the inner duality remained, with the potential for transformation to the original form.

Wood carving of a fish transforming into man. Tlingit, Alaska. (COURTESY OF THE
FINE ARTS MUSEUMS OF SAN FRANCISCO. GIFT OF ELEANOR MARTIN. 37764.2)

Experiencing a petroglyph rock as a transformed being is not
confined to time or to a particular tradition. AlixSandra Parness, a
clairvoyant and psychic, tells how she experienced a rock as a transformed whale at the well-known Seawolf petroglyph on Quadra
Island in 1996. (See Appendix Two.)

In the ancient tradition of the people of the Northwest Coast,
salmon lived in human bodies in their villages under the sea, but
transformed themselves into fish when offering their bodies as food
to humans. Then, being immortal, they were reconstituted in human
form from their bones, and swam back to their underwater villages.
So it was with wolves, bears, eagles and other species who lived as
humans just out of the sight of people.

Supernatural beings could remove scales, feathers and fur, and
transform, or partly transform, themselves from animal to human
appearance in an encounter with human suppliants who had ritually
purified themselves for the death-defying experience of the vision
quest, usually at the time of boys' initiation into adult life. Girls
quested less frequently. This was partly because of seclusion at the

time of menstruation and partly because the ordeals associated with quests of days, or even months, in the forest were thought to be too arduous for a female to live through. Spirits encountered on the quest became the youths' guardians. Such supernaturals often were terrifying, having the power to kill, but they took pity on initiates and bestowed upon them wealth, invulnerability or skills such as healing, canoe making, hunting and fishing. Amongst the Kwagiulth whose descendants are now living at Cape Mudge, initiates received songs and cries, rhythmic dance steps, costumes, masks and tokens to prove the authenticity of the encounter upon return to their community.

Tales of the ancestors' daring encounters with supernatural entities provide the subject for the most spectacular display of transformational art, the masked winter dancing. The youths depicted their spiritual journeys and exhibited the dual nature of the supernaturals they encountered by wearing articulated carved cedar masks. The masks might be great birds which opened to reveal human faces, or perhaps bear or wolf masks with human faces carved in the ears, or even sea serpent masks revealing human hands.

Dramatic performances of ritual theatre called into play all the arts: oratory, singing and drumming, masked dancing, painting of screens

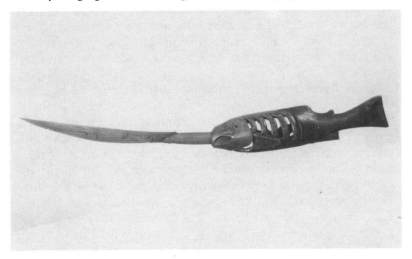

Ladle depicting dual forms of salmon. Tlingit. (COURTESY OF PHOEBE HEARST MUSEUM OF ANTHROPOLOGY, UNIVERSITY OF CALIFORNIA AT BERKELEY)

19

and elaborate paraphernalia for illusions such as flying birds, and the slaying and bringing to life of important dancers. Some of these dances are part of the present-day potlatch. Potlatches are reciprocal gift-giving feasts that display the privileges and wealth of the host family and secure their ranking position not only in their own village but also within the community of villages with whom they potlatch. Amongst the Kwagiulth, where the winter dances were highly developed into theatre, the whole community came to witness the transformational visions of a sacred nature.

Carved figures of fish transforming into humans are shown in early portrait carvings from the Tlingit of Alaska collected in 1898. The handle of a Tlingit ladle carved from one piece of wood represents the body of a salmon, whose exposed bones show the tiny, free-floating sculpture of a person inside. Salmon's transformation is elegantly portrayed.

b) Shamanism

The ideology of the transformation of life-forms, so important in the creative arts of the Northwest Coast, is part of a more general religious ideology termed Shamanism. The astounding vitality that kept the coastal rock-carving tradition alive over thousands of miles and immeasurable time is still felt in the arts of First Nations masters today. The arts are an expression of the ideology of Shamanism, which the great expert in this field, Mercea Eliade, has characterized as the world's first religion.

Native respondents have emphasized that care must be taken not to obscure regional variations by generalizing about Shamanism. What seems to be consistent in this ideology, however, is the acceptance of humans as only one population amongst many, with little qualitative difference between the lives of humans and those of other animals, and even inanimate beings such as rocks. All human and non-human persons were believed to have souls and be immortal. Powerful social animals such as bears and wolves, as well as elemental forces of nature such as lightning and thunder, were personified and portrayed as supernatural beings — not separate from ordinary life, but a part of the natural world and everyday experience.

It was the shaman's role to keep all these forces of humans and elemental nature in balance. For example, the dependence of coastal

"The Sorcerer," black-painted wall engraving, Trois Freres Cavern, France.
Paleolithic. (FROM BREUIL, *MEN OF THE OLD STONE AGE*)

peoples upon the salmon meant that the shaman was required to
assure that the runs came in. Greeting ceremonies were conducted
honouring the first fish caught (usually four).

The humans returned the bones to the sea intact after cooking the
fish and distributing the flesh. The bones were reconstituted and
given life again, restoring the good relations between fish and
humans. Keeping the skeleton of the fish together in an orderly way
was so important that in folk tales it is said that once, following the
First Salmon Ceremony, a little lame boy was seen hobbling along
the edge of the shore, and on into the sea. He was one of the ceremonial salmon. He had been honoured, but sadly, he was disabled by
the careless handling of his bones. Order was established, and good
relations assured, by strictly observing the rituals of interaction
between humans in their villages on land and humans in their villages
under the sea, who were transformed into fish in order to feed the
people on the land.

Photograph of Wolf Dancer, Koskimo, by Edward Curtis.
(COURTESY OF SPECIAL COLLECTIONS, UBC LIBRARY)

In the arts (including petroglyph art) of the Northwest Coast, bones, joints, skulls and ribs are prominent. This convention derives from the actual ceremonial treatment of animals in which the animal's bones were reassembled after death, in expectation of renewed life.

Communication with all life forms was maintained through respect and reciprocity, expressed in ritual. Cedar trees, for example, were formally addressed with reassurances of being left alive when sections of their bark were taken, and when berries needed to be picked the harvesters explained their need to the berry "boys" on the branches. All beings understood the language of humans, and responded to proper respect from them. Rigorous training was needed in order to become one with air, sea, earth and rock but the shaman had to enter into all those to prove his command of supernatural powers.

Deep within the Paleolithic caves of France, at least 30,000 years ago, engraved and painted herds of animals of huge dimensions were drawn on the walls, possibly as art for art's sake. It is more likely that they were drawn for ritual purposes by shamans. While it is not possible to determine the function of these great wall paintings and engravings, they are accepted as the work of shamans.

At Lascaux, a tableau suggests a direct connection to Shamanism. At the bottom of a deep shaft, difficult of access and deep within the cave, a stick figure, evidently human, lies stretched out as if in a trance. Beside him is a great bison, and near his hand lies a stick with a bird head on it. The bird in shamanic art is the definitive symbol of out-of-body flight.

This engraving has been interpreted as a shaman in trance, on a flight to the powerful spirit of the sky world, with a view to bringing in the herds of animals that are drawn and painted elsewhere on the cave walls. The geometric shapes, such as spirals, dots, zigzags, nesting curves and meanders, found in the caves at Lascaux in association with drawings of identifiable animal figures, are now being investigated to determine if they arise from shamanic visions in an induced trance state, such as can be studied in the laboratory with the controlled use of drugs like LSD. This kind of research makes it possible to compare such geometric shapes in rock-art images cross culturally, in various parts of the world, as has been done for the rock art of the San of Africa, the Shoshoni in the American Southwest, and elsewhere, including the rock writings in the Stein River Valley of British Columbia.

Shaman in trance state, Lascaux, France. (FROM POWELL, *PREHISTORIC ART*)

Shamanism, in a form which profoundly affected the ideology of North American Indians, was centred in East Asia and Siberia, and was described at the time of the first European contact with the aboriginal people of that area. As the last ice age ended in Siberia, ancestors of the present First Nations people followed the fish and great game animals across the Bering Strait land bridge and into North America. They brought their belief system with them.

Shamans of the North Pacific acquired and controlled the great powers of social animals such as bears, wolves, and whales, and a great variety of spirit helpers such as birds, sea serpents, and frogs. Supernatural beings became conventionalized in the arts.

It is the mastery of the techniques of ecstasy through an experience of death and resurrection from the bones that is the vital shamanic experience. This was associated with the ingestion of psychogenic plants in Siberia. Peyote and other plants are still used to induce trance today among some native North Americans. No drugs were used in inducing altered psychic states on the Northwest Coast.

Trance states in which visions were seen were achieved differently in the various societies along the coast, but in general they were produced by isolation, denial of bodily needs and ordeals of suffering on the quest for a spirit helper. This lonely trial of endurance took place in the forest during the winter months and was sometimes carried through year after year until a spirit helper was found. The need for food and water was ignored. Purification ordeals were undertaken, such as bathing in icy streams, or deliberate submergence in lakes for long periods. The body was whipped with branches of sharp-needled trees. At night, drained of strength, the seeker sang and danced around a small fire (itself of sacred significance) until he collapsed from exhaustion. Ultimately, having been reduced to a near-death state, the suppliant might have a vision of the spirit helper. The spirit helper encouraged, advised and remained with the person forever. It was a transcendental experience of ecstasy much the same as that of the monks in Europe who lived in unheated cells, kept silent, wore hair shirts and whipped themselves with thongs until the vision of a compassionate Virgin Mary appeared to them.

Tongues are significant in shamanic art. Power is transferred to a shaman by means of touching tongues with a supernatural spirit. (Shamans amongst the Tlingit and Haida collected tongues as amulets, especially those of river otters.) All these symbols — bones,

Tongued figure, L3. (NIGHT-LIGHT PHOTOGRAPH BY ROSS HENRY)

skulls, ribs and tongues — occur in petroglyph art, just as they occur in tradition-based contemporary art.

Shamans of the Northwest Coast performed a variety of functions, healing being of the utmost importance. They also controlled the weather, and the success of raiding parties. They prophesied, and claimed the powers of clairvoyance and the ability to cast out evil spirits and raise the dead. They carried naturally occurring faceted rock crystals in their sacred pouches. Tales tell of how crystals enabled them to fly, and how crystals pointed at an enemy caused death at a distance.

Shamans undertook out-of-body flights to the chiefs of the sky world, and had access to the land of the dead in the underworld to secure the lost souls of the sick. By these means they reinforced the community belief in levels of existence above and beneath the earth, concepts familiar in the world's later religions, which devolved from these primordial shamanic sources.

Feathers and down were used in costumes, and in various welcoming ceremonies, referring to flight to the upper world. Birds such as Raven and Thunderbird are symbols of contact with the sky world. Among the

SPIRIT IN THE STONE

Tsimshian, a shaman wore a crown of bear claws and a black bear robe during a healing ceremony. Bears were thought to have special power over the salmon, which the shaman sought to acquire.

Bears were often represented on petroglyphs in locations where shamans call spawning salmon up the river: for example, on Ringbolt Island at the Kitselas Canyon on the Skeena River. Consultation with the tribal Elders there elicited the information that the carvings depict shamans talking with the "chief of the Skeena" and master of the salmon, through bear spirit intermediaries. The ceremony at the rock carvings was intended to call the salmon runs up the river. Symbols of bear tracks are also found on the pitted rocks at salmon-spawning stations in the middle Fraser.

Shaman figure, Ringbolt Island, Skeena River.

The archaeologist George MacDonald has suggested that the descent to the undersea world to locate the oncoming salmon run was made through the ringed eyes of petroglyphs which represent the whirlpools formed by the river or sea. Under the water, shamans encountered Wealthy, known by different names in each language group along the coast. Wealthy controlled all the animals of the sea.

An upcoast artist gives the following description of a petroglyph site that brings together many of the ideas associated with rock-carving sites:

"One of my goals was to revisit the petroglyph stone in Forward Harbour that we [she and her husband] had discovered two years before with the help of Ray and Beth Hill's petroglyph book. This time we were able to tie to a rotting dock, in very shallow water, and spend the night. When we entered the harbour, pink salmon were leaping all over the bay and they continued to do so the entire time we were there. That palpable abundance coloured our stay.

"I headed for the petroglyph rock which is near the mouth of Wortley Creek. It is low and flat with a slight cant seaward. The rock is very dark and approximately six feet by 3½ feet in dimension. The upper surface is completely covered with incised outlines and eye holes. The largest carving seems to be a female figure with heart-shaped face, eyes, nose and mouth holes. The body is bulbous with a huge belly button giving the sense of a pregnant woman, and below that is what resembles an outlined vagina. Legs descend to block-like feet and vestigial arms fade into the rock at crude fingers. Strands of hair stand up from the head.

Female figure, Forward Harbour. (FROM A PHOTOGRAPH BY JUDITH WILLIAMS)

"I outlined the figure with water and discovered that a small natural fish-like formation above the head, if filled, would cause the water to flow down the hair and along the outlines of the body. This was a spirit of a place which the native people had been sensitive enough to recognize and delineate. The holes for the eyes were deep. In the one eye the visual field was filled with a lattice of prismatic hexagonal scales or cells sparkling and reflecting a spectrum of colour. It resembled the scales of a salmon. It was startlingly beautiful. When I stood up I noticed a nearby rock had an extrusion of sparkling faceted crystals.

"Looking at the carved rock again, I was able to see what seemed to be a supplicant figure at the knee of the large figure. There was a stylized animal head, rather like a bear, and from the head an upper and lower arm and 'paw' bent toward the female figure. The rest of the rock seemed to be covered with paired eyes with a few faces outlined. But I felt the figure, the salmon and the 'bear' were a complex, were what the place was all about. That was fecundity, a cycle of abundance, the salmon returning and spawning and the bear and other creatures feeding off the dead salmon."[15]

c) The Young Shaman

The undersea journey of a man with shamanic power is described in a Lekwiltok tale. The following is a simplified version of the drama which took place at the ancient Tsa-Kwa-Luten village on the high sand cliffs of Cape Mudge. The cliffs overlook the ceremonial rock-art site, described in Part Two. Island Comox speakers were in possession of the ancient village of Tsa-Kwa-Luten from earliest times until the southern advance of the Lekwiltok of the Kwagiulth Nation, who reached Quadra Island some 200 years ago. The names of the two contending shamans are Island Comox names. The structure of this tale, however, and its attribution are Lekwiltok.

Qa te nats, a youth from the ancient village of Tsa-Kwa-Luten, trained to become a shaman by bathing in a cold, fresh-water stream that ran beside his village. He was jealous of Qa te mo, a powerful older established shaman, because he was paid in canoes, princesses and slaves. He wanted to become a shaman himself and prove his superior power in a struggle to succeed his rival.

28

Figure of Sisiutl. Detail from the Don Assu dance screen made in 1979 for the opening of the Kwagiulth Museum at Cape Mudge. Gift to Assu by James Sewid. The screen was designed and drawn by Mark Henderson, and painted by Dora Sewid-Cook with the assistance of Adam Dick and Bill Reid. (COURTESY OF THE KWAGIULTH MUSEUM AND CULTURAL CENTRE, CAPE MUDGE)

He asked his younger brother to come with him, and together they went upstream to a place where a rock lay in the middle of the river. There the youth noticed a piece of bark lying on the rock and, feeling that it might be a sign to him, he sent his younger brother downstream to bathe in a separate place so that he might be alone. Every morning and evening for four days they returned to the river to purify themselves.

On the evening of the fourth day, the youth was startled by a strange noise on his return upstream to the rock. Something was moving in the salal bushes. He became afraid, and taking hold of the bark, he hurled it with great force into the bushes. The noise ceased. Though he did not know it then, the hidden being was Sisiutl, a terrible and dangerous sea serpent who could give shamanic power for curing the sick or paralyze the bodies of those not ready to receive such power.

Early the next morning the youth asked his brother to paddle him out to Mitlenatch Island; there he told his brother to return home with the canoe. He assured him that he would return. Then he descended by means of a kelp stem to the house of Komogwa (Wealthy), controller of the sea animals in the underwater world.

There were many shamans in the house of Wealthy, all of whom had tried but failed to relieve the pain in the side of Sisiutl, who lay there in human form. These shamans then asked the youth to attempt a cure. On feeling for the pain in the body of the "man," the youth felt the piece of bark which he had thrown while bathing, and sucked it out from the flesh. Immediately Sisiutl was relieved of his pain, and he praised the youth. He offered to help him become a great shaman. At once a power came into the house, and the young man fell into a trance. A lake appeared inside the house with reeds growing in it. A bird soared over the lake. But when the youth regained his senses, the vision was gone.

Meanwhile his brother, fearing that the young shaman was drowned, searched the beaches on the south end of the island near his village of Tsa-Kwa-Luten. When he finally came upon what appeared to be his brother's lifeless body, he found the young shaman still in trance, but alive. Together they returned to their father's house in the village.

Then all the people were called to witness the vision and curing powers of the young shaman. When he came among them in the house, a lake appeared with reeds growing in it, and a bird came soaring over the lake. Then power came into him, and he cured the sick. The rival shaman attempted to trick him and expose him as a fraud, whereupon the young shaman turned the situation to his advantage and destroyed his rival.

THE FIRST SALMON CEREMONY

There is a connection between petroglyphs and the ceremony greeting the first salmon of the year. In Oregon, a petroglyph with bear's feet was identified by the local people as a "rain-rock." "The upper surface is covered with a large number of shallow conical pits. The boulder was brought from the Klamath River to the Fort Jones Historical Museum in 1948. After it was brought to Fort Jones, a Shasta Indian stated to Mr. W. T. Davidson, County Supervisor, that, 'the rock had been used in the First Salmon ceremony since time immemorial until early January 1890.' In the fall of 1889 the salmon run was extremely late due to deficient rain and low water in the Klamath River, and the rock was 'uncovered.' Apparently it was ordinarily kept covered to prevent rain and a very great rain followed."[16]

The native people themselves have been characterized in ethnographies as "people of the salmon" in contrast to other North American groups dependent on bison, seeds or other resources. Their personal lives revolved around taboos and rituals associated with the salmon.

Twins are believed to be salmon people born to woman. They are given salmon names, and are called to take part in ritual dances and First Salmon Ceremonies even today.

An annual First Salmon Ceremony, a public event of the Northwest Coast and Plateau peoples and beyond for nearly as far as the salmon ranged, was likely the most ancient and widespread of all subsistence rituals. It has been suggested that the salmon ceremony is thousands of years old, and while other ceremonies have been lost through time, the rites to sustain the return of the salmon have lived on in several communities along the coast and in the eastern Arctic. The First Salmon Ceremony was always held for the whole village, though in modern times a sponsoring family receives prestige for sponsoring the ceremony.

The first spring salmon or sockeye salmon caught — usually the first four — were regarded as chiefs of the salmon people. Shamans are reputed to have seen the fish in their human form swimming in toward the seashore or ascending the rivers to spawn.

Almost all of the large, significant carvings on beach boulders along the coast are carved on the side of the rock facing the open water. Researchers to date have speculated that this is because the carving then relates to the life in the sea, and the powerful messages it conveys are taken out into the ocean on each tide. It should be noted, however, that the shamans who carved these symbols did so with

Salmon carving at Francisco Point, L5.

their backs to the water, facing both the beach and presumably the people for whom the ceremony was intended.

Calling in the fish runs took place as well at fishing places along the rivers, where shamans carved humanoid spirit beings, perhaps images of themselves, and figures of their spirit helpers, such as bear spirits.

In his work on the Salmon Ceremony of the Northwest Coast peoples, Alfred Kroeber mentions that amongst the Yurok of northern California, the words associated with First Salmon rites are recited in sections, mostly in dialogue, describing the origin of this ceremony by the spirits, as well as its immediate beneficial effects. Shamans speak before various rocks or spots that mark the abode of spirits.

First Salmon Ceremonies varied amongst different First Nations peoples according to their customs and propensity for simple or elaborate ritual. In general, the first fish were greeted with great ceremony, cooked and shared; then the bones, which were kept intact, were reverently returned to the sea. There they were transformed again into their human form and spread the news amongst their fellows that properly thankful people were anticipating their arrival.

The First Salmon Ceremony is carried out by First Nations people on Quadra Island today in the very place at Tsa-Kwa-Luten (L3) where 54 boulders with petroglyphs were once located. (Seven of the most outstanding petroglyph boulders were brought into the museum at Cape Mudge village for protection.) The great sand cliffs at the ancient village of Tsa-Kwa-Luten were undoubtedly a mystical place of significant spirit power. The likely time of year for the traditional First Salmon Ceremonies was late July or early August when the first great runs of fish appeared in Discovery Passage en route to spawning grounds on the Fraser River and its tributaries.

Modern First Salmon Ceremonies include drumming and oratory as part of the ritual. The association of the shaman with his drum is circumpolar, and as old as these sacred fishing rites. Perhaps the regular hypnotic sound of drumming on the rocks with another rock brought the shaman into a state of ecstasy. Drumming played an important role in inducing trance in the winter spirit dancing on the Northwest Coast. Perhaps the many rocks that are pitted but not otherwise inscribed with a recognizable spirit figure have been formed as a consequence of drumming, rather than having being intentionally created as such. There is a known link between drumming and the salmon ceremony.

The following event shows that drumming has an important link with calling in the fish in modern times. John Beal, a well-respected environmentalist in Seattle, organized the clean-up of the polluted Duwamish River and its tributary, Hamm Creek, after which he was approached by a Choctaw man who offered to drum the salmon into Hamm Creek to spawn. This person claimed that his people had used the ceremony for centuries. "After praying, the Choctaw man played his flute for a while and then began drumming."[17] He and a companion and Beal began walking up the river, drumming. Dorsal fins of fish could be seen heading into the river. "They followed us like pied pipers," Beal said.[18] When the drumming stopped, the fish would circle round and just lie there; when the drumming started again, the fish would get energetic and resume their way up the stream. A few fish had made their way up the stream since the debris had been cleared away, but the drumming ceremony made a significant impact on the number of fish that spawned in the river thereafter, and fry were in the millions.

As stated earlier, many diverse reasons for carving petroglyphs have been advanced by the modern descendants of the ancient petroglyph carvers, but the links with the First Salmon Ceremonies are compelling.

THE MYSTERY OF THE PITTED ROCKS

Deliberately pitted rocks have been somewhat overlooked by scholars writing on the petroglyphs of the Northwest Coast. On Quadra Island, petroglyphs with recognizable images caught the imagination of researchers while pitted rocks went undetected for many years. Nearly half of the petroglyph rocks found on Quadra Island have pits only. They are usually shallow, two or three cm deep, and about 5.8 cm (2") in diameter. Some are as deep as cups and bowls.

Shallow pits are often found on boulders alongside petroglyph carvings, along the coast and up the rivers. Pits are especially abundant upriver on the Fraser, and in Washington state along the Columbia River. On Quadra Island they are often found on the rocks that contain petroglyph figures, though usually there are several well-pitted boulders lying near a large figured boulder. The presence of a collection of pitted rocks almost always indicates that there will be a figured rock nearby.

Pounded pits in boulder, Tsa-Kwa-Luten, L3, in daylight.

Pits in the same boulder, by night-light.
(FROM A NIGHT-LIGHT PHOTOGRAPH BY ROSS HENRY)

Native people living up the Fraser River told James Tait that identical-shaped holes in boulders were made by male youths during the course of their puberty training. "He made round holes in rocks or boulders with a jadeite adze, which was held in the hand. Every night he worked at these until the holes were two or three inches deep. When making them he prayed 'May I have strength of arm, may my arm never get tired from thee, O Stone.' This was believed to make the arm tireless, and the hand dextrous in making stone implements of any kind."[19]

Along the Fraser River, petroglyph sites which include pitted boulders are found in the vicinity of important salmon-fishing places. A comprehensive survey of the Gibbs Creek petroglyphs on the middle Fraser (Prince George to Yale) in 1975 resulted in the detailed recording of 90 individual boulders, making this one of the largest sites presently known in British Columbia. "The site extends for about 1 km along the eastern shore of the Fraser River and from slightly above the present high-water mark to the low-water line. The majority of the boulders are submerged for most of the year, appearing during July and August when the river is low, at a time which corresponds almost exactly with the salmon-spawning runs. The site was and still is a great fishing station of the native people of the Fraser River area."[20]

At the Gibbs Creek site, the designs include heads, animal parts and random grooves, but the most common design is the simple pit which occurs singly, in pairs, in clusters, in rows and in other patterns. The many curvilinear designs at this site are similar to other rock carvings of the middle Fraser and of the Northwest Coast, many of which are also associated with fishing places. Some of the pitted boulders at the Gibbs Creek site may have been the result of arm strengthening done as part of the puberty rituals, but certainly, they have to do with the annual appearance of the fish and may have been pounded there by shamans as part of the ritual of calling in the fish runs.

Pits as vulvaform shapes, holding the waters of life and associated with the regeneration of life, have been a theme of research by Marija Gimbutas, of the University of California at Berkeley, who traces the hidden symbols of the female goddess in western civilization in prehistoric time. Michael Dames, writing about the stones of Ireland, called attention to the stone used to make the pit and the pit itself as a symbol of the united essence of deities as in lingam-yoni stones in India. There was no cult of the goddess, nor gods, on the Northwest Coast. Spirits were visualized mainly as stylized animal

35

forms, which referred back to myths. In the art, secondary sexual characteristics are rarely shown.

Wilson Duff of the University of British Columbia pointed out, however, that the act of making pits in rock may have given expression, more consciously or less, to the sexual creation of life: a cup shape holding water as the vessel of life and the phallic cobble, an image of male power. He likened the pairing of these two to the basic image of the human condition, like the yin-yang of China.

The interaction between the carver and the rock is actually physical as well as psychological. When pounded on granite, a naturally occurring cobble stone springs back into the hand from the rock in an elastic rebound, with a ringing sound. This would have provided accompaniment for songs sung by youths on the vision quest; their lonely cries and singing were heard and reported by early settlers.

Among the Shasta of northern California, shamans trained at certain traditional places and made rain by singing there. Pitted rocks in northern California and Oregon were associated with fertility and calling down rain. According to anthropologist Robert Heizer, "In the area where the distinctive Northwestern California type of civilization prevailed [Northern California and Oregon] practitioners of magic were, in Indian belief, able to influence precipitation almost at will. Rain making was associated with ritual at particular boulders."[21] The pits in these "sacred rain-rocks" resemble the pits in rocks found in British Columbia and elsewhere along the western coast of North America. Heizer quotes Harold Driver who mentions but does not describe Karok rain-rocks in the lower Klamath River area in Oregon: "Shamans trained at a certain rock near Katimin and ultimately make rain by singing there."[22]

Ellen White, speaking on rock carvings, mentioned the significance of pits on the moon as seen from Earth on the first moon-landing flight. "As they approached you could see the little puckered marks. Who went there? Not the body. Who was able to fly there? Not the body, but the soul or spirit, a gift from the Creator." Later she answered a question regarding pits on rocks: "In one of the stories, the Creator comes and he said, 'If you remember the many journeys to the moon, All Right! Heat up your hands.' They carve. They gouge. They take a chunk. They're used as a bowl to mangle dried food, medicines and stuff like that."[23]

Boulder bowls are located on Quadra Island at L2, L3 and L7. They are deep basins in otherwise unmodified boulders. They hold rainwater, and seawater on a retreating tide. One such bowl at the Kwagiulth Museum in Cape Mudge village (L2) is 43.1 cm by 45.7 cm (17" x 18") and 8.9 cm (3.50") deep. Beth Hill, best-known author to have written on the topic of petroglyphs, found boulder bowls at 26 sites associated with glyphs in British Columbia and Washington.

How these bowls were used can only be speculated upon. Among the Salish, the shaman washed his hands in fresh water before beginning a curing ceremony. Portable boulder bowls carved in the shapes of shamans and their power animals and forming a receptacle for water were used at puberty ceremonies for girls.

Water and sacred rites appear to be associated, as they are in many cultures; for example, baptism in Christianity and cremation at sacred rivers in Hinduism. Perhaps the shaman looked down into the water contained in bowls found at petroglyph sites as his doorway into the sea. This is symbolically expressed in the round spindle whorls used by Salish women on which the shaman is carved in the form of a bird spirit or other power animal. Like a whirlpool, this figure disappears into the spiral vortex when the spindle is revolved.

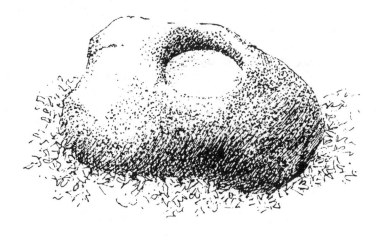

Bowl in a boulder, Kwagiulth Museum, L2.

37

Carved wooden Salish spindle whorl.
(COURTESY OF THE ROYAL BRITISH COLUMBIA MUSEUM)

Pits on rocks often appear to be random in distribution, but some pits form loops or chains which line up around the edges of the surface of a well-pitted boulder. In one case at Tsa-Kwa-Luten the pits are so numerous that they are not separately distinguishable, but form a beaten patina over the whole face of the rock.

At Francisco Point on Quadra Island, where dark gray biotite inclusions are found in the light-coloured granite in small jagged shapes like torn paper, the petroglyph maker has deliberately extended the apparently random pits in the area near a moustached head, as well as farther along the rock and on into the centres of several of these inclusions. Pitting into biotite inclusions is also found at Village Bay. (See descriptions of L5 and L10 in Part Two.)

The numerous rocks on Quadra Island which have been pitted only are found mingled with carved designs at major sites on the foreshores of ancient villages associated with fish traps, canoe runs and streams of fresh water. They most excite the imagination when encountered in a remote place. (See L9 in Part Two.) They may be found on a prominent boulder, at a site without other signs of past human activity. Some are on

Great pitted rock, Tsa-Kwa-Luten, L3.

offshore islets. Sometimes these isolated pitted rocks lie near giant boulders that can be seen from a great distance, themselves unmodified, which are thought of as "indicator rocks" because on Quadra Island, they often indicate that petroglyphs may be found nearby.

Examination by propane lantern revealed many more man-made pits on these rocks than can be detected in daylight. Those underneath great boulders would surely never have been seen otherwise, nor will they be seen again.

Pitted rocks on Quadra Island do not correspond to the orientation of figured rocks, where the image is carved on the sea side of the rock. They are usually on flat rocks without apparent orientation to the sea, or on a rock where the carver reversed the usual orientation and worked facing out to sea.

A remarkable discovery was made by Eric Harris, a surveyor, taking bearings while standing on top of one of the biggest boulders at L3. He noticed large pits on the top of a boulder well out to sea, far beyond where the other beach petroglyphs were found. The rock was only partly exposed on this occasion by the lowest tides of the spring. Later, a companion rock, similarly pitted, was found nearby.

Petroglyphs underneath a great boulder, Tsa-Kwa-Luten, L3. (FROM A NIGHT-LIGHT PHOTOGRAPH BY ROSS HENRY)

(See Part Two for information on these hidden rocks in the context of the site at L3.) The high sand cliffs above the beach have been eroding at an average rate of about 28.5 cm (1.0') per year. Two hundred years ago, when Tsa-Kwa-Luten, the village on top of the cliff, was occupied, the shoreline would have been 60 m (200') farther out to sea. Since the coastline of this area changes so dramatically, it may be that other petroglyphs lie underwater farther from the shore. Frequently, it is the unusual circumstances in which the pitted rocks are found that adds a sense of mystery to them.

THE IMAGERY: CONVENTIONS OF CONTENT AND STYLE IN PETROGLYPH ART

Ritual work in stone expresses the very heart of Northwest Coast spiritual life and art, bringing an image of the spirits from the unseen world into reality. Rock carving has ancient roots indeed, and in its presence we sense the dream world of the artist as it developed in the rainforests and rugged coasts of the Pacific Northwest. Most coastal art is huge, as shown by the size of houses, memorial poles, storage boxes, canoes and masks. Petroglyph art of the Northwest Coast also tends toward the monumental. The petroglyphs may be found on smooth rock walls or wide sandstone shelves on the beaches. Boulders chosen for rock art are usually large, relative to those lying about them on the beaches, with the images uncrowded on the rock surface, and the image itself of a generous scale.

Petroglyphs from widely separated geographical areas of the coast share subject matter as well as conventional ways of depicting eyes, fingers, hands and geometric symbols. Humanoid spirit figures are found everywhere; less frequently, birds, wolves, salmon, bears and whales are depicted. Often there are designs of a mysterious nature that suggest visions. Petroglyphs are an early variant of classic Northwest Coast style. An exhibit in 1995 at the Canadian Museum of Civilization in Hull, Quebec, illustrated the continuity of style in works of stone, bone, wood and fibre from a 2,000-year-old village site in Prince Rupert harbour into this century.

While a few sub-styles in petroglyphs have been recognized by scholars within specific culture areas along the coast, Vancouver Island and Quadra Island are within the "Basic Conventionalized Style" area which stretches from Siberia, along the Northwest Coast

Figure distinguished by heavy eyebrows, Tsa-Kwa-Luten, L3.

Head of frog sculpture in wood by Tahltan-Tlingit artist Dempsey Bob.
(PHOTOGRAPH BY HAROLD DEMETER)

to the Columbia River, where a different style is distinguished. The basic style is essentially the same as historic Northwest Coast art known from wood and argillite carvings and from paintings. This basic style in rock carving is curvilinear, with circles and smoothly connecting lines. Human and other animal forms have internal details shown, such as tongues, ribs and backbones. The distinctive feature of wide, arched eyebrows is used almost universally on the faces of humans and other animals from ancient to modern art; indeed, it is so characteristic of the art that it seems to be a culturally shared requirement for defining "face." It is one of the features that permits the identification of art as coming from this region.

Tongues in the art are particularly significant, for by means of tongues the power of the spirit was passed from supernatural beings to shamans. Basically it is the passing on of this connection to the spirit world which has provided the energy for the amazing continuity in the arts of this immense area.

In some cases, artists working on petroglyphs carved the facial features first. This is confirmed by an unfinished carving on Quadra Island, where

Figure with angular protrusions, L3.

Unique snout-like protrusion on a different rock at L3.
Evidently the vision of the same carver.

the features are complete, but the groove outlining the head is not; it ends in a line of pits clearly intended for a grooved extension.

Some glyphs are dramatic, with angular protrusions jutting out from a head, giving the whole an aggressive appearance. One in particular at L3 with a unique, snout-like protrusion is awe-inspiring. Has this spirit vision been inscribed on more than one boulder at the same site? Surely the snout-like appendage on the composite carving could only have been conceived by one mind, probably executed by one person. Other instances of more than chance similarity of images have been noted.

The natural unevenness of rock, and the energetic work required to bring an image into being on tough granite, result in portrayals that are simple and powerful, yet inventive. While many images along the coast evidently derive from each carver's traditional subjects, many surely come from their powerful and unique visions.

Limbs are frequently shown attached directly to the head. The upraised arms may symbolize the healing power generated in dance movements or speakers' gestures, as suggested by artist Roy Vickers of Tofino.

Kwagiulth women today spiral with arms raised as they appear from behind the dance screen at a potlatch, and their raised arms in

Carved face with arm and hand attached to head, Tsa-Kwa-Luten, L3.

Figure with limb attached to head, Kwagiulth Museum, L2.

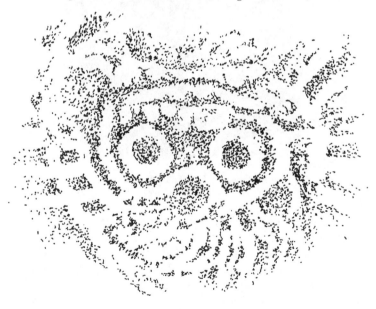

Mask-like face, Tsa-Kwa-Luten, L3.

45

the dance, like those seen on many petroglyphs on Quadra Island, may, as mentioned, represent the healing power of dance. This in turn suggests that some of what we are seeing in the carvings is the representation of spirits danced in the sacred winter season.

Specialists in the study of the Amur River petroglyphs, where heads appear strikingly similar to some of the heads carved in rock on the Northwest Coast, regard them as representing masks. Some authorities here believe that the Northwest Coast petroglyphs might also represent masks. The size of the petroglyph heads, mostly a little larger than life-size, could suggest that masks were used as models.

Contemporary owl mask by Bob Cranmer.
(COURTESY OF THE MUSEUM AT CAMPBELL RIVER, 17345)

It is unlikely that all heads represent human beings. A good number of them depict birds, the shamans' familiar, indicating astral flight, with tufts on the head, pinions, and even eggs between the legs.

Spirit faces and heads are frequently shown in petroglyph art as they are in the general art of this extensive coastal area. Wilson Duff, anthropologist and specialist on images in stone, wrote, "Artists of the Northwest Coast were obsessed with faces.... There were human

Bird figure with egg, Tsa-Kwa-Luten, L3.

Two spirit figures on one boulder, Kwagiulth Museum, L2. Attenuated arms may be bird pinions. Style suggests two figures by the same carver.

47

faces ranging from simple stylizations devoid of expression to realistic portraits, serene or savage. There were faces of men possessed, and of spirits, and animals and supernatural creatures as grotesque as the mind can conceive."[24]

In petroglyph art, attention is focused mainly on heads, which are carved with depth and clarity, while body parts receive minimal attention. The heads are presented from the front and are laterally symmetrical. Both these conventions are features of the carvers' art of the Northwest Coast, past and present. In a figure at the Kwagiulth Museum, what appears to be a deeply carved female image shows head, breasts and vagina with only a simple, tentative grooved line along one side; however, these shapes may be unconnected symbols grooved upon the rock. They might possibly have even been carved at different times.

Female figure, Kwagiulth Museum, L2.

Many outlines of heads, in Quadra Island rock art, especially at L3, are ovoid in shape — a rounded rectangle or bean-shaped figure. This is the most characteristic design unit in Northwest Coast art. At L1, a naturally occurring bulge in the shape of an ovoid, on an otherwise

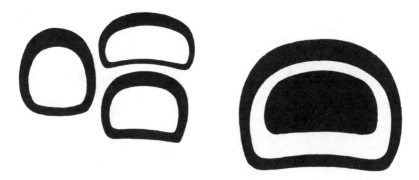

Ovoid shapes.

flat face of rock, was completed by running grooves out from the significant symbol. At L3, a prominent, 19 cm (7.5") in width, dark gray-green inclusion in the shape of an ovoid can be seen on a light gray boulder. Beside this ovoid is the well-known bird with egg carving. After some 20 years of speculation on the possible significance this shape might have held for native people, a rubbing was made and an eroded face appeared within the ovoid and a deep groove that had been carved to encircle it. Under the face are legs and bird feet, and below the feet is a big egg. Another rubbing was made farther along the rock and another figure was discovered. Neither figure can be seen with the naked eye. Since the ovoid was less in use in the art of the southern Salish, it suggests that the petroglyphs on Quadra Island may have been carved by the Kwagiulth. Both Salish and Kwagiulth occupied the northern Strait of Georgia region and Quadra Island sites at different times. Part Two discusses the possibility that this and other motifs in the art might indicate which people carved the individual glyphs on Quadra Island.

Many petroglyph figures along the coast have been described as human because the structure of the face and head is human in shape. In Northwest Coast art, projections and decorative elements were, and still are, added to this basic shape, to identify the specific spirit being portrayed. This is analogous to the masks of the 19th and 20th centuries from the central and northern coast, where human-shaped heads are distinguished by beaks, paws, snouts, teeth and fins to indicate which of the supernatural spirits of the animals are being portrayed in the masked dances and on memorial poles. Ordinary animals were considered to

Rock with protruding ovoid shape, L3. (PHOTOGRAPH BY ROSS HENRY)

Figures on the rock shown in the photograph above.

have souls and they gave themselves freely to the food supply. A supernatural being revealed itself only to those on spirit quests where it transformed part of its animal body into its human counterpart.

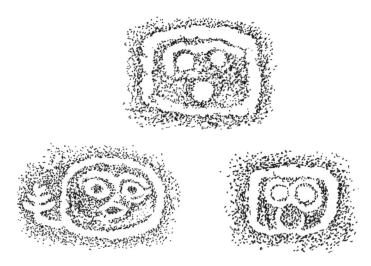

Three petroglyph faces in ovoid shapes, Tsa-Kwa-Luten, L3.

As well as representative images, indecipherable elements are occasionally seen in petroglyph art. These may derive from the mental images perceived by shamans in certain altered states of consciousness. Concentric circles, for example, are thought to represent the vortex actually experienced in both ancient and contemporary psychogenic experience. Amongst coastal petroglyphs, there is considerable input of an enigmatic and exotic nature that may have derived from a vision experienced by the artist carver in a state of spiritual transcendancy.

Petroglyph art, unlike traditional European painting, does not ordinarily organize the elements of multiple portrayals of birds or other spirits found on one rock face into a scene. This expressive art is concerned not with the exterior landscape but with the inner meaning of the symbols portrayed. Where multiple images are carved into the rock they do not necessarily create a picture. They may have been inscribed at different times, as space and time permitted.

On petroglyphs, as in small portable sculptures found in early archaeological excavations on the Northwest Coast, naturalistic figures

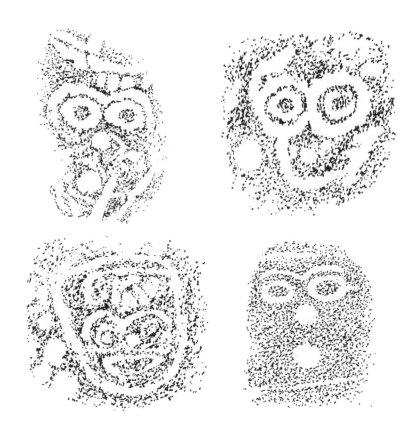

Carved faces from several sites.

of whales, birds and fish were sometimes carved, often in their most easily recognizable form: that is, as seen from the side. These representations became stylized so that with but a few features, the carver's intention to show the attributes of a certain spirit being is recognized. From the ethnographic and archaeological record it has been deduced that the essence of these portable carvings is the spirit power of the animal, made available to the carver. The small sculptures could be worn as amulets or kept wrapped with other objects of spirit power.

What appear to be moustaches, heavily grooved beside the mouths on a number of faces of human or sea creatures, suggest that one important spirit is being represented. Such deeply carved heads are found at three major sites on Quadra Island, on prominent boulders.

A moustached face at Francisco Point, L5.

Carved eyes at Francisco Point, L5.

53

Eyes formed by spirals, concentric circles or pits in circles are the focus of the face. Two deliberately made pits in a rock suggest eyes which could animate the power in the boulder. It is the eyes that are noticed first, for they are likely to be deeply carved. Where the shamans once stood or squatted to create these eyes is where the observer is standing now — a circumstance that has had a powerful effect on many people. These people say they feel an intimate connection to the carver and the carver's visionary spirit.

There is more to these stone eyes than just eyes. Concentric circles for eyes may represent whirlpools, which were an entry into the rich

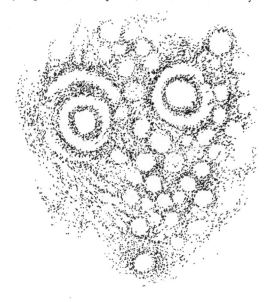

Eyes in pitted rock, Tsa-Kwa-Luten, L3.

undersea world, a portal of descent for the shaman who called in the annual runs of salmon. This view of the shaman's descent through the rock was made graphic by Ellen White of the Nanaimo Band when she described the energy by which the shaman was able to cleave the rock and enter through this gap into the sea.

Dyan Grant-Francis, a psychic from Victoria who worked with Beth Hill, has given a dramatic account of a visionary experience at the petroglyph site at Kulleet Bay on Vancouver Island: "I 'saw' an Elder sitting at the edge of the rock where I was kneeling. He sat alone at the beginning, gazing into the bowl, seeking guidance. He wore cedar cloth and there were few trees around the bowl at that time, it being closer to the beach than it is now. I heard these words to begin the story:

" 'When we gaze into this bowl we are drawn into the sky, flying in brotherhood with the World to find the reasons for our tribe's misfortune, or how we can call the whales back to our beach after the cold. It is our gateway, the opening between these worlds into which we can fly. We dive into the sky from this bowl edge. We are the guardians of this gateway, and we guide and protect the shaman during his flight...all worlds flow to one.' " (For more detail see Appendix One.)

On Quadra Island, there is a boulder shaped like a raven's head. This auspicious form apparently spoke to the petroglyph maker for, among other figures on this rock, the most outstanding are a skull-like face carved where the "eye" of the bird would be, and two deep pits pounded into the "beak" for nostrils.

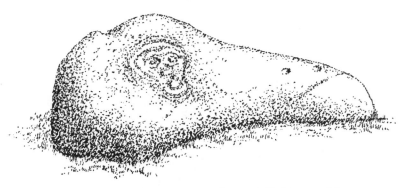

Boulder shaped like a raven's head, Kwagiulth Museum, L2.

Rocks with suggestive shapes, at various locations on the Northwest Coast, were seen to be transformed animals, including humans, even the shaman carver himself. This phenomenon gave special power to the rock which evidently influenced the carver in its choice.

Petroglyph boulders are often found on Quadra Island in a group of rocks on the beach that look like sea mammals basking. In 1985 at L3, a group of such boulders was investigated. On close examination of a seal-shaped rock, a perfect man-made pit was discovered on top of the "head." The "saddle" of the rock appeared to be abraded, and

Seal rock and associated pitted boulders, Tsa-Kwa-Luten, L3.

Rock shaped like a whale, L3. (PHOTOGRAPH BY ROSS HENRY)

could have served as a seat for the petroglyph maker who pounded deep pits into an adjacent boulder. Iron salts have stained the holes in the big boulder a brownish-red. Another rock in this cluster has faint pits running down the "spine." These rocks might have been chosen because they were perceived as transformed mammals.

Another great boulder at L3 is shaped like a whale. Big pits run all the way down the "spine" of this rock, and down the middle "tail" section. Night-light reveals a myriad of smaller pits down both shore side and sea side of this "whale." (See Part Two, L3.)

The Seawolf rock at L7 is shaped like an orca (killer whale). As well as the major design, it has large pits running down the "spine," and a well-defined natural "flipper" on its landward side. (For a clair-voyant reading at this rock see Appendix Two.)

THE TRADITION

Contemporary First Nations artists work in the great tradition of their ancestors who created the carved images found in archaeo-logical sites, the petroglyphs, and the splendid 19th- century art that is the treasure of the world's museums and art galleries. Most of the great masters of Northwest Coast art today were born in the remote villages of their people. The world view that generated the arts of this area lingers in the minds of the grandparent generation in native communities. Native languages, still spoken by the oldest generation in coastal villages, structure the thought of the Elders who advise the youths, particularly grandchildren, so that the mystique of the ancient beliefs is still alive. Contemporary artists do not borrow from the past so much as capture mythic reality in their imaginative work. Occasionally, the actual symbols of petro-glyphs appear in the work of today's masters, but of greater importance is the physical collections of Northwest Coast art with its ancient, rich heritage of shamanic symbols upon which First Nations artists rely for creating new works. Northwest Coast art, as a whole, retains its vitality from the immemorial images of the spirit world.

Recognized First Nations artists train carvers in their own schools of art; most carvers apprentice to masters working in the styles of their own nations along the coast. In 1997, 182 native-owned and -operated enterprises in British Columbia showed and sold native art. Some of

Human and bird figures, painted by Shane Point in the style of an earlier house board from Nanaimo. (COURTESY OF THE NATIONAL MUSEUM OF CIVILIZATION)

these enterprises interpreted the culture of their people through arrangements of traditional costumed dances as well as demonstrations of cooking, especially the barbecued salmon staked over outdoor fires. Carved masks, paintings, prints and other items are sold to an international clientele.

Artists working in Northwest Coast styles have incorporated various modern techniques, applications and stylistic influences of other traditions into their productions. There has been an on-going exchange of techniques and styles between the native and non-native communities of artists. Jack Shadbolt, a non-native artist renowned for his entranced manner of painting, credits coastal Indian art as the source of his inspiration: "All in all, it is a complex, ongoing relationship which has developed between us for which I acknowledge my debt with gratitude."[25] American artist Barnett Newman, whose transcendent work "Voice of Fire" hangs in the National Gallery in Ottawa, liked to say that Kwagiulth art served as his teacher.

Some First Nations artists have produced two-dimensional paintings and silk-screen prints intended to be viewed from the front, and read upwards into the retreating space of perspective, in the European tradition.

Susan Point, from Musqueam, B.C., has developed banners inspired by spindle whorl designs of her Salish ancestors, designs which resemble figures in the petroglyph tradition.

Roy Vickers, a Nisga'a artist living at Tofino, has incorporated petroglyphs on the rocks in his landscape paintings of unspoiled rain-forest and sea. His paintings are peopled by the Elders of past ages, and contemporary figures. In the background are the ancient symbols of his people and images derived from his own personal spiritual experience. One female figure from his "Eagle — Full Circle," used as a logo for his enterprises, especially resonates with the spirit and style of ancient petroglyph art.

Pam Holloway, a Kwagiulth artist from Campbell River, has used petroglyph designs carved into clay in her impressive tile assemblages. The damp clay is first grooved with a petroglyph design, then dried and fired. The grooves are then painted in gold and the tiles are refired, burnished and assembled.

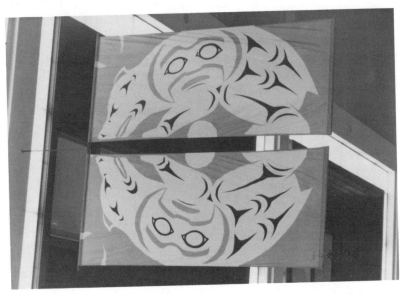

Banners by Susan Point, Vancouver International Airport.
(PHOTOGRAPH BY GERRIE DINSLEY)

Detail from "Eagle — Full Circle," painting by Roy Vickers.

Carved and painted clay tile by Pam Holloway. (PHOTOGRAPH BY PAM HOLLOWAY)

60

Greg Colfax of Neah Bay, Washington, created "The Prophet of Direction," for a poster entitled "Origins," in 1989. In it we see the use of petroglyph art in the work of a modern master. The petroglyph symbolism was intended by Colfax to draw attention to the oneness of the experience of First Nations, as expressed in the rock carvings of ancient ancestors, rather than to their separate variations on a theme, nation by nation, so often emphasized by academics and other specialists in the arts of the Northwest Coast. Colfax feels that too great an emphasis has been placed on the "wanderings" of Northwest Coast peoples. In reality, they moved from place to place, under whatever circumstances, deliberately, according to the prophetic instructions of their shamans, to the settlements where they have resided now for thousands of years.

Increasing numbers of knowledgeable buyers have fueled the market for Northwest Coast art in the past 30 years. Superb works in the old tradition by the great masters are sought after worldwide by both individual collectors and corporations, and many are priceless. Robert Davidson, a Haida artist, has remarked,

"Origins," poster by Greg Colfax.

61

"throughout our history, it has been the art that has kept our spirit alive."[26] It is significant that the great bronze sculpture, "Spirit of Haida Gwaii," by the Haida master Bill Reid, carries its crew of humans and supernaturals on into the 21st century, and for centuries to come.

"The Spirit of Haida Gwaii," sculpture by Bill Reid.
(PHOTOGRAPH BY BILL MCLENNAN)

PART TWO

THE RELATIONSHIP OF QUADRA ISLAND PETROGLYPHS TO FEATURES OF THE SITES WHERE THEY ARE FOUND

Nearly a hundred carved boulders at 13 sites have been located to date on Quadra Island. Part Two illustrates and describes petroglyphs at 11 locations where intensive work has been carried out by our research team: locators, Marcy Wolters and myself; surveyor, David Smith; mapper, Nancy Allwarden; geologist, Malcolm Campbell; photographers, Ross Henry and Julie Campbell. Six more petroglyph boulders at three additional sites have been located recently. These have not been studied in depth, nor yet reported to the Archaeological Sites Branch, and are not included in the descriptions of the sites that follow.

Ninety individual rock features have been studied at the 11 sites with reference to each other and to their setting. Forty-four petroglyphs have spirit figures depicted on them. Forty-six have pits only and four of these are generous bowls ground into the tops of boulders.

First Nations people have been living at the site of Cape Mudge village, now a reserve, for approximately 2,000 years, plus or minus 150 years, by radio-carbon dating. This is within the possible range of time in which preserved petroglyphs are said to have been carved, according to archaeologists Lundy and Carlson. People may have lived

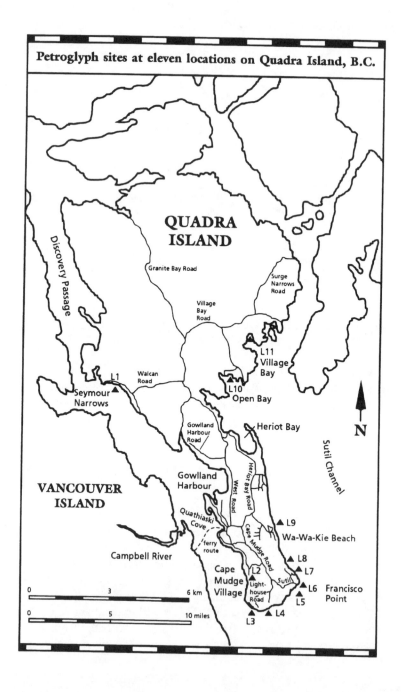

Petroglyph sites at eleven locations on Quadra Island, B.C.

for a still longer period at other ancient Quadra Island village sites where archaeological excavations and dating have not been done. A date of 2,000 years is a logical possibility for dating these petroglyphs, but unlikely, given their erosion on beaches swept by surf.

Both Salish and Kwagiulth peoples have successively occupied the villages on Quadra Island. The northern Strait of Georgia was Salish territory until the Kwagiulth entered the region in the 1790s. The Salish, once as far north as Port Neville, moved southward as far as Bute Inlet on the mainland, and the Vancouver Island Salish moved from Sayward as far south as Comox. The Lekwiltok, southernmost bands of the Kwagiulth, were settled at Cape Mudge by the 1850s. Archaeological sites on Quadra Island have been assumed to be ancient, and hence have been attributed to the Salish. However, a rock carving was made by the Kwagiulth at Fort Rupert on Vancouver Island as late as the 1850s and other petroglyphs could have been carved on Quadra Island at about the same time, or shortly after. It is likely that both the Salish and the Kwagiulth made the petroglyphs of Quadra Island.

There is no sure way of determining which are the oldest carvings, and which are more recent. The style and subject matter of petroglyphs on Quadra Island seem to compare most closely with rock-art designs from the old Salish territory that once stretched as far north as Port Neville, yet the Kwagiulth themselves had a village in Port Neville over 200 years ago, and could have been the carvers of the more recent petroglyphs located there. Petroglyphs at Bella Coola, an outlying Salish-speaking enclave some 400 miles north of Quadra Island, strongly resemble the Cape Mudge petroglyphs.

In a general way, the images on the petroglyphs of Quadra Island seem to relate more closely to those in the old Salish regions to the north, than to those on Salish-held islands and other territories to the south. There are, however, a surprising number of faces done in a grooved, bean-shaped outline (ovoid), especially abundant at L3, suggesting a relationship in style to the art of the northerly tribes of Kwagiulth, Haida and Tlingit, rather than to the Salish. Other features indicating sources of Kwagiulth imagery are discussed in the descriptions of some of the Quadra Island sites.

It is possible that the older petroglyphs, i.e. those most eroded, were carved by the Salish while those with deeper carving, presumably more recent, could be attributed to the Kwagiulth. However, the evidence cannot be definitive since the original depth of the pits and grooves, and the relative rate of erosion by the sea at each site, are not known.

In one location (L1), the rocks on which the petroglyphs are carved do have a dark patina and the outer surface is crumbling, giving the appearance of great age, because of deterioration. However, acid effluent from the nearby pulp mill across Discovery Passage has probably affected the appearance of the rocks and defaced these petroglyphs.

Carvings on the rock face at Open Bay (L10) are barely discernible and give the impression of being very old. The "Orion" figure at L8 has grooves worn so smooth that it is difficult to see with the naked eye.

One panel of petroglyphs at L3 is so eroded that the carvings were only seen under extraordinary circumstances, such as the first light of

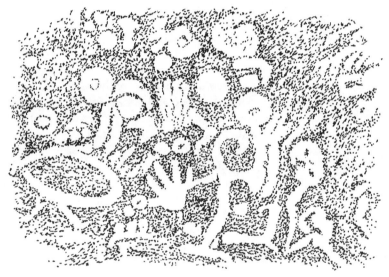

Eroded panel of figures at Tsa-Kwa-Luten, L3.

dawn. Also, faint markings on the undercut face of a huge boulder at L3 were only seen by propane lantern light, suggesting a greater antiquity than seems to be the case for most others at that site. If relative erosion can give clues to attribution, L3 and L5 may have been used for rock carving by both Salish and Kwagiulth, since both almost-invisible carvings and deeply carved designs are found at each of these sites.

The moustached head at the base of the Seawolf rock at L7 was located by chance while a researcher was rubbing over an area of pecked pits. If the antiquity of a petroglyph could be determined by the degree of erosion, this would be a Salish carving. Deep cups in the stone run over the "spine" of the rock and along all the sides. One set of pits is in the arrangement of the five dots on dice, a set that could easily be converted into a face by grooving between the lower pits to form a mouth. The simplicity of this set of pits and the eroded state of almost all the pits on this rock make it appear that they are older than the well-preserved Seawolf design on the seaward face. The northern and central coastal iconography featured in the Seawolf design, such as the characteristic eye-shape and the internal rib structure, make it a definite candidate for Kwagiulth attribution. However, one can only speculate. Both peoples made petroglyphs in the basic and widespread style that prevails over nearly all of the central coast.

Petroglyphs made thousands of years ago have almost certainly vanished because the boulders on which they were carved lie on the beaches, open to wave action and the cracking of their surface by frost during winter. Erosion has been accelerated in the last 30 years, with driftwood from logging hurled against these rock artifacts in winter storms. Acid in the air and sea has taken its toll. Indeed, many of the petroglyphs illustrated in this book will never again be seen with the unaided eye, even in the most advantageous light, because erosion continues to smooth out the pits and grooves of now-faint images. This evidence connecting the First Nations carvers of the Pacific Northwest to their spiritual experience is washing away in the sand.

Some carvings may be glimpsed when shadows fill their pits and grooves in a low cross-light at dawn or dusk on a clear day, especially after a light rain. Many were discovered at night, however, with the intense light of propane lanterns, a method used successfully by David Walker and his associates.

Research on the petroglyphs of Quadra Island is something of a salvage operation, recording images that are fleeting. Many of the illustrations of petroglyphs in this book were drawn from photographs of rubbings made with black wax on cloth of those petroglyphs already discernible only by night-light.

Rock carvings are significant cultural landmarks of First Nations peoples and are protected by law.

The numbers and letters in brackets on the location maps have been assigned by the Archaeological Sites Branch, Ministry of Tourism, Small

Business and Culture, Victoria, B.C. They are keyed to latitude and longitude as a geographical locator for reported sites across Canada.

LOCATION 1 (L1)

There are seven petroglyph boulders at this site on the west side of Quadra Island where the Morte Lake stream empties into Discovery Passage. On the flood tide, as the water moves southward, a jet breaks free and flows along the shore at L1, creating a strong backwater. L1 is located where rivers of salmon once poured through the gap of Seymour Narrows and into Discovery Passage in summer, en route to the Fraser River spawning grounds.

The upland above the beach has not been developed. It is private property. This level bench was the site of the ancient and historic village of Kawstin. It is possible to beach boats on a wide, sandy shore; guides must be familiar with the local waters.

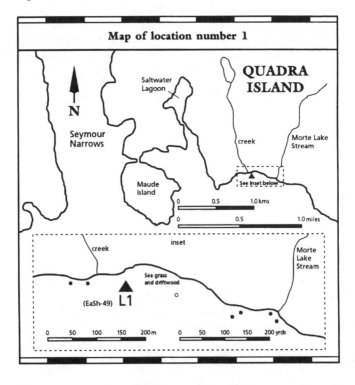

Petroglyphs here, as at other sites on Quadra Island, are found in the intertidal zone on large boulders left by melting glaciers approximately 15,000 years ago.

The petroglyphs are difficult to see because of weathering and possible acid-rain corrosion from the pulp mill on the Vancouver Island side, across Discovery Passage.

Regular pits on boulder near outlet of Morte Lake stream, L1.

All but one of the rock carvings are close to the bench above the beach, within 28 m (91') of the piled driftwood and grasses on the upper beach. By contrast, one significant petroglyph boulder is farther down the beach towards the water, 43 m (141') from the driftwood. It seems to occupy a central position relative to the others, and may have been a focal point for petroglyph ritual as viewed from the village.

The prominent rock is flat-topped. It is bigger than the other petroglyph rocks at this site: 2 m long by 2.5 m wide (8.2' x 6.6'). A thick vein of quartz, 3.81 cm (1.5") wide, runs through the granite. An indistinct but significant feature is a circle formed from two shallow concentric rings. It is the largest petroglyph circle found on Quadra Island, and the only one with a set of double grooves. It is

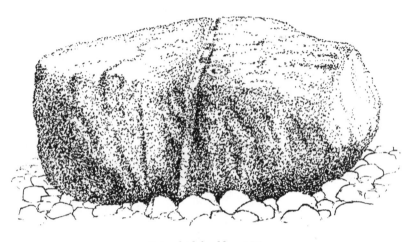

Petroglyph boulder at L1.

15.2 cm (6") across. This ring lies just beside the quartz band, and close to the top edge of the rock in front of which the carver would stand if the rituals performed were intended to be viewed by the inhabitants of Kawstin village. The ring is lighter in tone than the rest of the rock because the quartz crystals in the granite have been shattered by the pounding required to produce it. Some irregular pits have been pounded along the quartz band. The whole flat top of the rock shows evidence of pitting at intervals.

The big shallow ring may symbolize the dangerous whirlpools in the sea offshore. A shaman making the ritual journey through a "Shamans' Doorway" in this place had much to contend with in an encounter with the master of riches in the sea. The rage of waters in the narrows must have been an awesome hazard to the people of Kawstin through the centuries. (Thirty feet of Ripple Rock pinnacles blocking the passage at Seymour Narrows were blown off in 1958.) The nature of the location may have dictated its use for secret shamanic training, initiation and public First Salmon Ceremonies.

According to Harry Assu, a fisherman and respected Elder, born in 1905 at Cape Mudge village, "There was a place where dangerous sea monsters were often sighted. Right in Seymour Narrows. We call that place 'U'stoy. One of these monsters always emerged around Maude Island. It must have been fifty feet across and always above its body, which looked like a great skate, there were little birds swirling round and round on the water. Everybody stayed away for fear of being dragged in and pulled under the water."[1]

One remarkable petroglyph at L1 seems to fit Harry Assu's description. Circular rings are found around the perimeter of a flat-topped, 1.0 m (3.3') boulder across which there are long grooves resembling bird forms.

Other rocks show simple pits, and one a humanoid face. One boulder has a naturally formed protrusion on it, ovoid in shape. A groove has been dug around this significant shape, which is a basic formal element of Northwest Coast art. Other grooves run out from it, and there are single circles on this rock as well.

The people of Kawstin knew the waters so intimately that they took their dugout cedar canoes through the narrows at slack tide. First Nations peoples on this coast have been characterized as "people of the salmon" and as the "canoe people." There is an array of 40 to 50 clearings for canoes fanned out in this one bay. The rocks that were cleared away to provide a pathway for canoes form long lines from sea to shore. These rocks once served to weigh down poles over which the canoes could be dragged without damage to their hulls, which were burnished to reduce friction while being paddled.

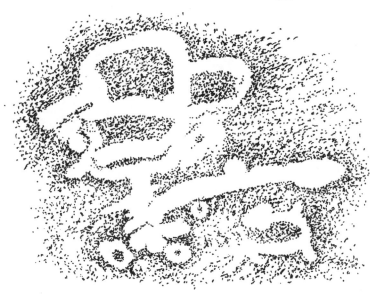

A naturally occurring ovoid protrusion with carved extensions, L1.

71

LOCATION 2 (L2)

L2 is the museum site in the First Nations village of Cape Mudge. This collection is comprised of seven of the petroglyphs from L3, Tsa-Kwa-Luten (DlSh-1), which were brought in to the village in 1972 to protect them from erosion on the beach and from vandals. In addition, one boulder was brought in from the beach north of the village. (EaSh-33). These petroglyphs were amongst the best known at the time, and are outstanding by virtue of their deep carving and large figures.

Four petroglyph boulders, including a stone bowl, are beside the ramp in front of the Kwagiulth Museum and Cultural Centre. Another four rocks with carvings are placed in the open area between the houses on the foreshore, across the road from the museum.

These eight carved boulders are the most accessible to the public. They are best viewed in low light at early morning or late evening when shadows fill the pits and grooves. The museum occasionally arranges a guided night tour for the public. Propane lantern light is

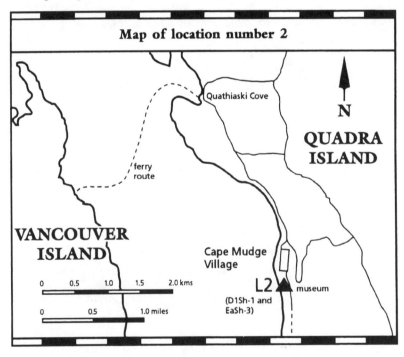

Petroglyph at Kwagiulth Museum, L2.

Petroglyph at Kwagiulth Museum, L2.

used to bring out not only the prominent carvings but also otherwise unseen figures on the tops, sides, backs and projections of the rocks.

Rubbings by the public are not permitted by the Cape Mudge Band at this location, or at Tsa-Kwa-Luten (L3). The museum has fibreglass moulds of island petroglyphs from which rubbings may be made. Original oil-on-canvas rubbings may be purchased by arrangement with the Kwagiulth Museum and Cultural Centre.

LOCATION 3 (L3)

At least 54 boulders with petroglyphs were originally on the beach in this location. (Seven rocks with carved figures were moved from this site to L2, the museum at Cape Mudge village.) Of 47 remaining, 22 petroglyph boulders are figured, and 25 have man-made pits only. Two of these latter are bowls in boulders. The Tsa-Kwa-Luten site is the most abundant petroglyph location on Quadra Island. It can be reached by car. The public is invited to park

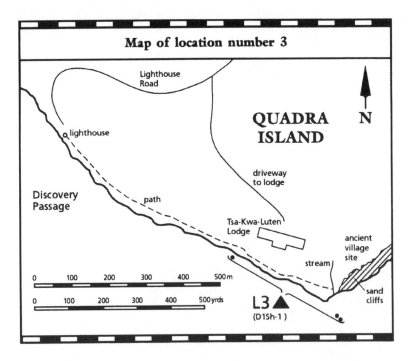

Drawing by John Sykes of the old Tsa-Kwa-Luten village, 1792.
(COURTESY OF THE MINISTRY OF DEFENCE, ENGLAND)

at Tsa-Kwa-Luten Lodge, a fishing resort of the Cape Mudge Band, and to visit the resort while touring the petroglyph site.

The distance along the beach from the lighthouse is 550 m (1800') southeast to the first petroglyph boulder, directly below the major resort buildings. The area with petroglyphs stretches from there for 365 m (1200') along the beach in the intertidal zone towards Point Mudge, to just beyond where a fresh-water stream flows onto the beach at the side of high white sand cliffs.

The awe-inspiring nature of the cliffs no doubt contributed to the spirit power of this place for shamans who had the responsibility of calling in the great riches of the sea. Just offshore is renowned salmon-fishing ground.

Atop the approximately 31 m (100') cliffs at Cape Mudge once stood the big village of Tsa-Kwa-Luten, visited by Captain George Vancouver and his crew in 1792.

Boulders with petroglyphs become more and more numerous on the beach from where Tsa-Kwa-Luten Resort now stands to where the ancient village was located on the heights. This suggests a connection at this site between the village and the petroglyphs, and perhaps the public nature of petroglyph ritual for the benefit of its inhabitants.

In this location there is an outstanding rock, 2.4 m by 3 m (8' x 10'), with a sea lion or walrus-like figure on a pitted surface that

Carved face with arm and hand attached to head, Tsa-Kwa-Luten, L3.

covers the whole face of the boulder. Shamans would have pounded the sea side of the rock, while facing an audience on shore. This appears to be the important ceremonial centre at L3. The huge petroglyph rock may be thought of as associated with another great rock beyond it, 3 m by 1.8 m (10' x 6'). They are on either side of the remains of a rock fish trap, much disturbed by surf. The second rock is pitted only, though a low boulder near its base has two heads grooved on it. This is the last petroglyph boulder at L3.

The sandy area between these great boulders is also significant in that it provided the last passage out to the sea. Beyond is a river that forms within the tidal pools and pours out of a single gap into the sea. It would not have been possible to launch canoes through the tidal pools below Tsa-Kwa-Luten village at low tide except through this portal.

There are no petroglyphs at L3 past this point, suggesting that ceremonies at these petroglyphs were associated with the First Salmon and the launching of canoes. Many of the petroglyphs along the beach at L3 are associated with the rocks used to weigh down the poles of the canoe skids. Petroglyph rocks are often grouped at the high end of the sandy runways lined by these rocks.

Two petroglyph rocks were discovered far out in the water between the two huge boulders described above. They are nearer to and probably associated with the figured one, and in line with the canoe passage between the boulders and out to sea. They are only exposed at the lowest spring tide. These outlying rocks were located by surveyor Eric Harris who, standing on the last prominent rock at L3 and looking out to sea, observed a line of pits on the ridge of a submerged rock, as attached robes of seaweed washed back and forth over the top. Later the companion rock was discovered nearby. These rocks are lavishly and deeply pitted. If these are drumming rocks, their location in the area for launching canoes at low tide could have been significant for shamanic ceremony, probably the First Salmon Ceremony.

One particularly distinguished rock at L3 is an ample boulder, 2.43 m by 1.82 m (8' x 6'). It is shaped like a whale or dolphin as seen from the shore side, and is somewhat lighter in colour than the surrounding rocks. Big pits are visible at regular intervals all along

Pam Holloway in her "whale" button blanket beside the boulder shaped like a whale, L3. (PHOTOGRAPH BY JULIE CAMPBELL)

the length of the "spine" of the rock and over the "tail." Lantern light revealed many more pits from the ridge of the rock down the sides. They are especially numerous on the side facing the sea.

Figure distinguished by heavy eyebrows, Tsa-Kwa-Luten, L3.

There are so many fine petroglyphs at L3 that it is not possible to describe them all. Some are illustrated in Part One. Petroglyphs on these boulder-strewn beaches are difficult to locate, even for those familiar with them. Some illustrations in this book give a delicate rendering of visions from the spirit world that will not otherwise be seen again.

LOCATION 4 (L4)

The figure cradled on the rock at L4 was the only petroglyph known at this location for many years. On the assumption that where there is a symbol carved on a rock, there are likely to be deliberately pitted rocks nearby, a search was carried out and a pitted rock was found 56.7 m (186') in a westerly direction from the figured rock at roughly the same distance from the driftwood on the shore. The pits are in dark sandstone.

78

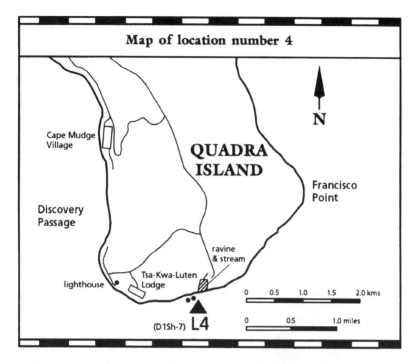

Map of location number 4

N

Cape Mudge Village

QUADRA ISLAND

Francisco Point

Discovery Passage

ravine & stream

Tsa-Kwa-Luten Lodge

lighthouse

0   0.5   1.0   1.5   2.0 kms

0   0.5   1.0 miles

(D1Sh-7) L4

The local name for the figured rock is "Salmon Man." Some of the great appeal of this rock carving lies in the fit of the design to the top of the rock on which it is carved. Also, the smiling face is unique and appealing. Generally speaking, the up-turned or down-turned mouth in Northwest Coast carvers' art does not portray happiness or sadness. However, the smile makes this figure engaging to anyone seeing it today. Arms, legs, ribs and genitals are depicted.

The location can be reached by boat under favourable conditions at low tide, but it is difficult to make a landing along the rocky shore. The best route is to walk from the lighthouse around the southern tip of Quadra Island for 1640 m (one mile).

The Salmon Man carving is located 274 m (1000') west of a seasonal fresh-water stream that has formed a ravine in the cliff. It is 25 m (82') towards the sea from the vegetation and drift-wood. The carving is on a granite rock, 0.85 m (3') long, 0.4 m (1.3') wide and 0.35 m (1.1') deep. There is no other indication of native use of this site. The land above the beach at L4 is private property. The high sand cliffs have slumped over the driftwood line, so that any evidence of human occupation that might have been observed on the bench above the sea has been obliterated.

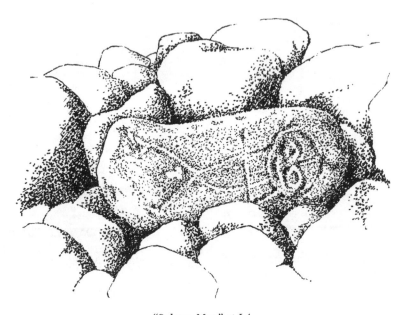

"Salmon Man" at L4.

It is purely speculative, but tempting, to associate this petroglyph figure with the tale of "The Young Shaman" told in Part One. In the mythic story, the initiate's entranced body was washed up on this shore, after he received shamanic power from the two-headed serpent, Sisiutl, in the house of Wealthy, master of the riches of the undersea world, whose house was below the kelp beds off Mitlenatch Island, 12.4 km (6.7 nautical miles or 7.7 miles) offshore at this site. Because of the tides and currents here, it is in this area of the south beach where, even today, searches are initiated for bodies washed up after drownings.

LOCATION 5 (L5)

Thirteen boulders with petroglyphs have been located in this area. Many of them are pitted only, and of those which are figured, most relate to fishing.

L5 can be reached by walking south from the beach access at Petroglyph Road to a brass survey marker reading "Francisco Point" on a boulder 2 m (6.5') in diameter by 1 m (3.28') high. This rock with the survey marker is high up the beach, often in driftwood. The distance from Petroglyph Road to the brass marker is 534 m (1752'), and from the marker to the first petroglyph rock is 183 m (600'). The petroglyphs are found mostly on the larger clustered rocks farther south. Though the area where the petroglyphs are found is marked on the map, the individual positions of carved boulders is not marked, at the request of the upland owner.

Francisco Point can be reached by boat. A wide clearing for rowboats and gas boats was made in the 1930s by summer squatters

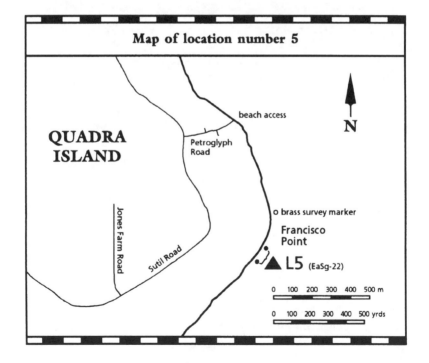

Map of location number 5

on the land who sold fish to B.C. Packers at Quathiaski Cove. This boat runway probably covers the old canoe runs. The cluster of petroglyph rocks on the beach is nearly in line with the boat clearing. Well-known salmon- fishing grounds are offshore.

Moving from north to south, the first petroglyph encountered is pitted; the next is a spirit with bear-like ears on a small oval stone.

Nearby, on a great boulder, is one of the most intriguing petroglyphs at L5. It shows two large circular faces, known locally as "The Twins" or "The Lovers." These large, carved heads are just touching. The arms are intertwined and leaf-like fingers can be distinguished. The foreheads show design markings. The linked faces and arms may

Two joined faces, "The Lovers," at L5.

depict twins, widely regarded by coastal peoples as salmon born to woman. Twins were given salmon names, and played a part in public rituals to call in the salmon. There is a less-defined face higher up on this rock with one outflung arm and hand. Man-made pits and grooves occur on this boulder in profusion.

82

Rock shaped like a sea lion, with faces, at L5. (PHOTOGRAPH BY JULIE CAMPBELL)

The rock itself is shaped like a sea lion as seen from the bench above the sea. It is 1.5 m in height (3.9'). The length is 2.5 m (7.54') and width is 1.5 m (4.9'). The rock is 20 to 30 m (66' - 98') down the beach from the vegetation on shore. The granite is lighter in colour than the surrounding rocks. The orientation of the figures and pitting on the side of the rock are unusual in that the ritualist would be standing with his back partly toward the shore, though still clearly visible by people gathered on the beach terrace for witnessing the ceremony, probably the First Salmon Ceremony. The land above high tide is now private property. There is a fresh-water spring at this elevation and indications of early occupation by First Nations which are now much disturbed.

Nearby is a rock on which faint, head-like grooves are no longer discernible to the naked eye, but the rubbings with black wax on cloth suggest an aberrant moustached head. Lower on this same rock is a faint design of eyes, brows and tongue in the same configuration as the splendid design at L2.

Owl-like eyes once stared from the side of a flat rock that has been turned by the wave action to a position under the "fish-

Natural pool shaped like a salmon at L5. (PHOTOGRAPH BY JULIE CAMPBELL)

Head on the "fish-pool" boulder at L5.

84

pool" rock, described below, so that this petroglyph can no longer be seen.

Perhaps the most fascinating of these carvings is on a granite boulder, 1 m by 2 m (3.28' x 6.56'), with what appears to be a natural pool nestled in the mounds on top of the rock. The salmon-shaped pool fills with rain and sea-spray, and is often covered with pink to red algae. This natural salmon shape did not go unnoticed by the carver. An elegant head is portrayed beside the pool, with hair or a headdress lying at its rim. To carve this petroglyph, the shaman would have had to stand with his back to the water and face the shore, as is the usual orientation.

A low, flat rock with faint pits over the surface is located close beside and at the base of the fish-pool boulder. Pits are lined up around part of the rim of this rock, indicating that the ritualist was aware of the form of the rock while pounding the pits.

The last petroglyph at L5 lies farthest south, 23 m (75') from the driftwood. A bold carving of a head with prominent moustaches is on the southernmost end of the rock. Three faint fragments of visages, with eyes and top-of-the-head ridges have also been distinguished, as well as one with the upper portion of a head groove, and eyes, brows, mouth and tongue. They are near the split end of the rock that contains the bold head.

Many pits are pounded into this rock, apparently at random. However, in some cases where there were dark surface patches in the gray granite, a deliberate selection was made by pounding into the centre of some of these dark biotite inclusions. This selection is evident on another petroglyph rock at Village Bay (L11).

Early peoples have left evidence of settlement at this site in the charcoal-black earth and crushed shell of midden soil on the bench of land that runs parallel to the beach. Fresh water was available on the bench, now private property. Rituals at any of the petroglyph sites on the beach would have been best observed from this elevation, with the focus on the fish-pool rock as central to the site.

LOCATION 6 (L6)

To reach L6 walk 370 m (1214') south from the beach access at Petroglyph Road toward Francisco Point. One skate-shaped petroglyph boulder is found at this location. The rock is small for a petroglyph rock: 0.75 m by 0.5 m (2.46' x 1.64'). There are two pits on the "spine." What may look like a third pit is a natural cavity. There are fractures in the rock, which is 20 m (65') from the vegetation on the shore. Midden soil, evidence of native occupation, is found at intervals in this area all along the bank above the shoreline. What may be a much disturbed clearing of rocks for launching canoes is found in association with the pitted rock.

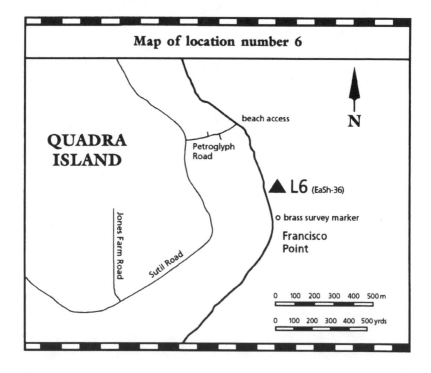

Map of location number 6

QUADRA ISLAND

beach access

N

Petroglyph Road

▲ L6 (EaSh-36)

o brass survey marker

Francisco Point

Jones Farm Road

Sutil Road

0   100   200   300   400   500 m

0   100   200   300   400   500 yrds

Pitted rock at L6.

LOCATION 7 (L7)

L7 is 185 m (607') north of the beach access at Petroglyph Road. There are four boulders altered by pitting and grooving at this location. It is known that a habitation site existed nearby because the bench above the beach is blackened by ancient campfires and filled with crushed shell. There is a spring on the bench above the first petroglyph boulder, and native people said that the petroglyph was there to mark this spring. According to pioneers, the spring is capped, and the well is now on private land; there is also a stream 55 m (180') from the fourth and last carved rock, bearing 150 degrees.

A series of tidal pools fronts the site. Barriers of rock were assembled between them so that families could claim the fish left by the retreating tide. The Seawolf petroglyph is the best known (often the only one) of the Quadra Island petroglyphs. It has been described by petroglyph specialist Ed Meade as "a little work of art."[2]

The Seawolf design symbolizes the combined attributes of whale and wolf and is usually portrayed in art with a salmon caught in its tail. In a circumpolar myth, Wolf and Whale are one creature. When the footprints of wolves disappear from the sand into the sea, whales return. The combined powers of the greatest hunter of the land and the greatest hunter of the sea gave powerful magic for fishing.

The Seawolf carving is always partly visible because of the dark lichens that grow in the pits and grooves. The whole rock may have been conceived of as a transformed whale. The boulder is high in the driftwood line. The side facing the sea, on which the image is carved, is concave, so that it is partly protected from driftwood dashed against the rock in winter storms. Many pits of varying sizes, some

Seawolf at L7.

unusually deep, are visible on the rock, including some prominent ones pounded along the ridge of the rock. Invisible pits have been recorded by rubbing with black wax on cloth. This technique revealed a head with moustaches amongst the pits on the "spine" of the rock near the base.

A pecked and ground bowl, 60 by 40 cm (24" x 16"), in a large boulder which now lies on its side is found 23 m (75') northward from the Seawolf at the rim of the tidal pool. It may be associated with ceremonies at the Seawolf rock since shamans in this Strait of Georgia region were known to wash their hands in fresh water before beginning important ceremonies having to do with puberty rites for girls and for curing.

An intriguing figure was located in 1997 on a rock that showed no more than tiny chips on the face. It lies northward from the Seawolf on the inner shore of the tidal pool. Two rows of tiny pits outline a familiar style of head with headdress and what appears to be a tongue. Legs run down from the head. Perhaps the person who worked upon the design of this rock did not return to complete it since many pits have not been further grooved into channels. The

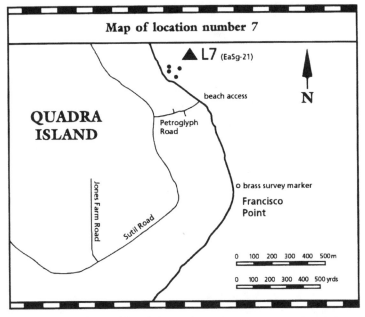

Map of location number 7

image is on the shore side of the rock so that the carver faced the sea. This was the first petroglyph rock encountered on Quadra Island to have this orientation. It is just 8.3 m (27') from the next petroglyph and they rest on either side of a clearing for canoes.

Two visible heads with tongues, and two heads not visible to the unaided eye, are carved on a 0.5 m (1.5') high rock, 86 m (282'), bearing 150 degrees, from the Seawolf. The low, dark, diorite rock has two smooth and sloping panels, one toward the land and one toward the sea. It is 1.2 m (4') long and is the second rock so far described to have the major carvings facing the shore instead of out to sea. The grooves under the mouths of the four faces may be lip ornaments, as proposed by Beth and Ray Hill, best-known authors on coastal petroglyphs. The intention of the carver cannot be known, but as tongues are a major theme in rock art on this island, these may well be tongues.

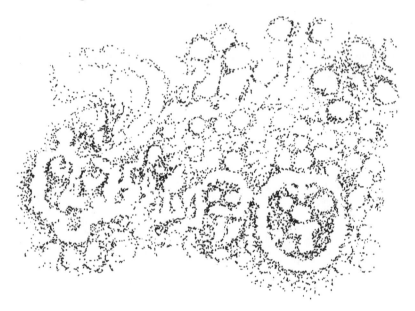

Tongued heads at L7.

The rock described above also has neatly formed and regularly spaced pits on the side facing the water. Since this rock and its near neighbour are on either side of the only undisturbed canoe run, which is opposite the gap in the offshore reef, it reinforces the notion of a ceremonial launch of canoes from shore at this point. A fresh-water stream enters the sea 55 m (180') beyond this petroglyph rock.

LOCATION 8 (L8)

L8 lies approximately midway between Petroglyph Road and the Wa-Wa-Kie area on the east side of Quadra Island. Best access to the petroglyphs on the beach is along the Kay Dubois Trail, which starts

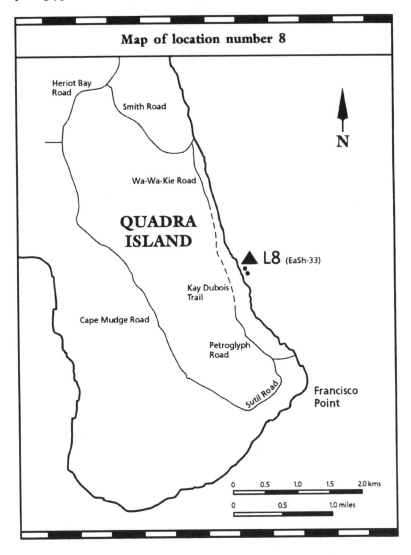

Map of location number 8

Heriot Bay Road

Smith Road

N

Wa-Wa-Kie Road

QUADRA ISLAND

▲ L8 (EaSh-33)

Kay Dubois Trail

Cape Mudge Road

Petroglyph Road

Sutil Road

Francisco Point

0   0.5   1.0   1.5   2.0 kms

0   0.5   1.0 miles

past the settlement at Wa-Wa-Kie and ends at Sutil Road. The trail crosses a stream that flows out into Otter Bay (a local name). In years past there was considerable midden soil deposit on both sides of this stream, and a wide clearing on both sides that suggested ancient habitation.

The petroglyphs are found most easily by walking the trail to the biggest rock on the beach in this area. The location is near the south end of the trail leading to Sutil Road. This big rock is rounded on top. It is 2 m high (6.56') by 4 m in diameter (13'), and sits 30 m (98') below the vegetation at the high-tide line.

North of this boulder by 68 m (223'), there is an "indicator" rock, so-called because of its marvellous sculptured shape, which could not go unnoticed over the thousands of years of occupation by native people. This would probably be considered a sacred place, indicating shamanic work on stone nearby. The indicator rock is 1.3 m high by 1.5 m in diameter (4.26' x 5') with two apparently natural deep smooth channels on the sea side, one of which ends in a shallow bowl.

The powerful impression made by this sculptured boulder prompted repeated visits there in the hope of finding petroglyphs

Indicator rock at L8.

associated with it. After many years, one was revealed: a singular impression of a person spread out upon a rock. It is 19.5 m (65') north of the indicator rock, pitted and grooved on a stone 0.4 m high by 1.4 m in diameter (1.3' x 4.6'). It resembles the configuration of the constellation of Orion which is visible in the southern sky from this location in winter. Its mouth is uniquely moon-like. It is more spindly, spare, and diagrammatic than most known petroglyphs here and along the coast, so it may be a more ancient style of representation. The figure is so eroded as to scarcely dent the rock upon which it has been grooved.

Figure spread out on rock at L8.

The body points due east, out to sea. The carver worked with his back to the shore, suggesting it was carved without an audience in mind. The constellation Orion was recognized in myth by societies around the northern hemisphere and was thought to be a hunting or fishing scene, useful for fishing magic.

One other petroglyph rock was found at this site not far from the figure described above and at nearly the same distance from the shore in a northwestward direction. It is pitted at intervals on both its land

and sea sides, and has a ring carved on the sea side as well. It may be significant, in relationship to the "Orion" petroglyph, that the rock itself is black with mottling of mica, which makes the whole thing glitter in the sunlight like stars. This rock, from which a rubbing was obtained, has never been found again, despite repeated searches over several years.

Location 9 (L9)

The most impressive petroglyph at L9 is on the beach north of the public access road at the foot of the hill at Wa-Wa-Kie. It is 654 m (2146') north of the public car park. The pitted rock lies just 2.4 m (7.87') beyond the biggest boulder encountered en route. This big indicator rock was visited many times before a petroglyph was discovered. The dimensions of the big rock are 2.6 m high and 4 m in diameter (8.5' x 13'). It is 18 m (59') from the driftwood line.

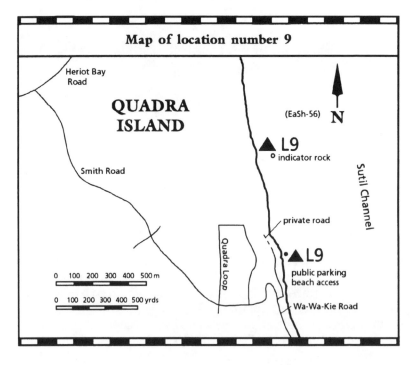

Map of location number 9

The petroglyph rock is at roughly the same distance from the drift-wood line. It is 0.5 m high (1.6'), with a diameter of approximately 1 m (3.2'). Pits cover the face of the boulder on the shore side of a dark granite rock. Thus the petroglyph maker was facing out to sea. The pits in the rock suggest drumming, hence this location may have

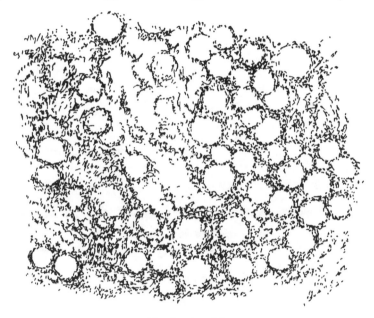

Pitted rock at L9.

been a sacred place for drumming up power on the spirit quest. The carver must have been meticulous in the sizing and the spacing of the pits, which are perfectly lined up and conform to the edge of the rock on its right side.

The nearest fresh-water stream is 362 m (1188') southeast. Behind the driftwood in the forest there is a wide clearing which may have at one time served as a campsite.

Experience had shown that where there is one petroglyph, there are probably others. The site at L9 was revisited many times. A second find was made closer to the stream at the foot of the access road at Wa-Wa-Kie. The rock is a rounded, light-coloured granite with a solid white line. It is 0.5 m in length, 0.5 m in width, and 0.4 m high (1.7' x 1.7' x 1.3'). A head with moustache can just be distinguished upon the top face of the rock. The shoreline at this point does not offer any distinguishing mark; however, there is a single evergreen on the high-tide line, at 111 degrees from the petroglyph rock at a distance of 28 m (95').

LOCATION 10 (L10)

Three petroglyphs are found at L10 on a basalt rock face approximately 9 m (30') high that slopes into the sea. Lava has intruded into sedimentary beds of siltstone and limestone, changing the beds in places into eroded pits and whorls of rock of intriguing form. Some of the rock carvings are covered at high tide, and access at any time is by boat only. Sand beside the cliff provided a place to beach a canoe on this rocky shore.

The figure and a single ring are near the base of the rock just above the sand. Higher up there are meanders and grooving. Near the top of the rock face are fake petroglyphs: little ships pecked with tiny pits broken through the darkened cortex. According to the Archaeological Branch, they are not made in the bold technique of

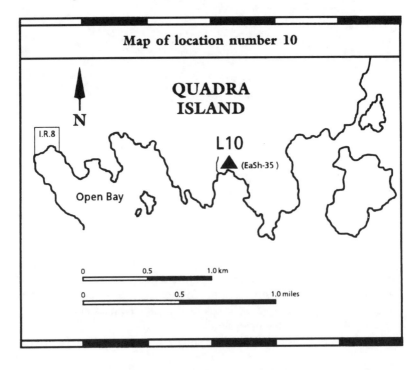

Map of location number 10

QUADRA ISLAND

N

I.R.8

L10

(EaSh-35)

Open Bay

0   0.5   1.0 km

0   0.5   1.0 miles

Figure at L10.

genuine petroglyphs and are thought to have been made by workers long ago in a limestone pit nearby.

There is a seasonal fresh-water stream about 12 m (40') west of this site. Extensive shell-heaps are found in an adjacent inlet at the head of Open Bay, where a big village was once located.

LOCATION 11 (L11)

The petroglyph rock at L11 is on the main shoreline of Indian Reserve 7. Access is only by boat. The petroglyph rock is north-north-west of the little island at the entry into Village Bay. An old trail that led down from Village Bay Lake to the shore is now on private property. Only seven of many deliberately made pits are visible on a sea-scoured outcrop that meets the sand at high-tide level. Fragments of darker rock (gabbro) have been deliberately pitted, as in a rock at Francisco Point, (L5). This petroglyph rock is located west approximately 38.8 m (127') from the point where the sand and gravel beach ends and bedrock begins. The rock is fractured and underlies a

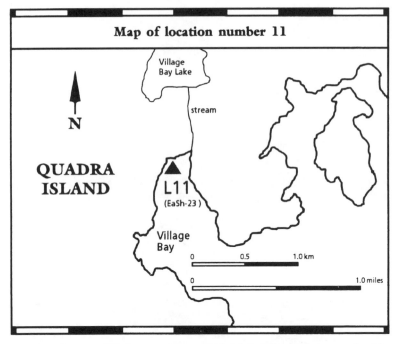

Map of location number 11

Village
Bay Lake

stream

N

QUADRA
ISLAND

L11
(EaSh-23)

Village
Bay

0   0.5   1.0 km

0   1.0 miles

massive diorite cliff about 6.09 m (20') high. The rock is porphyritic microgranite. The pits are strung out along 102 cm (40") of rock face. Drumming on the rock for singing may have produced these pits.

The nearby Yakwin River flows out of Village Bay Lake. It is likely that the ceremony at the petroglyph was intended to bring in the salmon which school offshore in fall before entering a pool at beach level and ascending the river to spawn. Petroglyph drumming on the rock and other ritual acts by shamans, who had the power to control weather, may have been intended to cause rain so that the spawning salmon could ascend into the lakes. Amongst many of the tribes of northwestern California, where the Northwest Coast culture influenced society, rain-making was associated with rituals at particular boulders. The consequence was pits in these "sacred rain-rocks" that resemble the pits in rocks found here and elsewhere along the western coast of North America.

Smoking salmon for winter use on the beach where the petroglyph rock lies is still remembered by Harry Assu, an Elder of Cape Mudge village today. According to Indian Affairs Branch records of 1906, the Wei-Wai-Kai Band at Cape Mudge had built a fish ladder at the mouth of the river. Human occupation over thousands of years is suggested by midden soil on the trail from the lakes just inland of the beach on reserve land and by more midden soil at the fishing station on the east side of the river near the mouth.

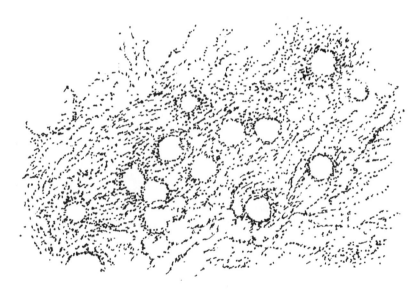

Pits on rock at L11.

Development has done little to disturb the immediate landscape and seascape at ten of the 11 petroglyph locations described. The natural world where the petroglyph ceremonies took place looks today much as it must have looked to the carvers of the petroglyphs and those who took part in the rites associated with the petroglyphs.

The mystery of the sacred is sensed in these places where once people gathered to celebrate their sense of connectedness with all the elements of earth, sea and sky, and especially with the salmon, for it was upon the regeneration and return of the fish that their lives depended. Here shamans marshalled all their knowledge of the visible and invisible worlds, whose sacred nature required a proper and respectful equilibrium between humans and all other forms of life. It was in these places that the sacred spirits were carved in stone.

APPENDIX ONE

Beth Hill often consulted Tom, whose psychic power had aided archaeologists from Egypt to Australia. Once, on his apprehension of imminent danger, Beth and another companion fled from the petroglyph called the "Shamans' Pool" at Kulleet Bay near Ladysmith. This natural depression in the sandstone is ringed with carved faces and Beth learned that it is used by the present inhabitants of a nearby village for bathing in its icy waters during the rigours of initiation into winter dancing. It was reported by C. F. Newcombe of the B. C. Provincial Museum in 1931 that, "The old chief of the Kulleet Bay Band...thought that [the carved heads] had probably been executed by ancient Shamans during their initiation, part of which consisted of prolonged fasting; the carved figures represented those seen in dreams."[1]

Beth returned on another occasion with Dyan Grant-Francis of Victoria, a psychic who has a Master's degree in sciences. Dyan has worked in archaeological research in the Northwest Territories; over a span of ten years she was closely in touch with the Inuit and Dene peoples there. Fascinated by the oral traditions of native peoples, Dyan studied Shamanism and shamanic traditions for approaching the spirit world. Her experience at the Shamans' Pool took place in 1995. It was fall and the leaves had turned their rich autumn hues. She describes the experience in her own words.

Beth and I drove through the village at Kulleet Bay and down an almost obscured dirt track into the trees. We got out of the car and Beth began to walk farther into the bush. I noticed an energy field surrounding the site, a tangible "veil" of energy that, as we walked through it, was like a cloth of soft tingles against our skin. Beth felt this energy field also. Even before reaching the bowl, I could see a circle of Elders, shamans in their ceremonial capes of painted cedar bark, some short, others long, and painted hats of various designs which I described later and drew for Beth. The circle was incomplete, with more people on one side than the other. This turned out to be the same distribution as the faces carved in the bowl. As we reached the actual bowl I still had no idea what to expect as Beth had told me little about this petroglyph site. Beth began to clear away the fallen maple leaves, a carpet of gold covering the carved stones and filling the depression of the rock.

I knelt at one end of the bowl and began to "open" to the spirit of this place, of this sacred site. A rather menacing figure began to form at the opposite end of the bowl and grew into a towering form, a spirit of immense proportions which loomed over us and roared. It was more than a human image, more than any earthly image I could conceive. Realizing that an offering was needed, to show respect to this spirit and the profound history of this site, I ran back to the car in search of something appropriate and found dates — sacred food in the Middle East. I began the chant which would call the spirits of the four directions. I laid the dates at the edge of the bowl, speaking of our intention that day, to contact the spirit of the bowl, and our desire to honour this place.

Once the protective spirit was appeased, the doorway opened and I was flooded with visions and voices telling one story of the Shamans' Pool.

I "saw" an Elder sitting at the edge of the rock where I was kneeling. He sat alone at the beginning, gazing into the bowl, seeking guidance. He wore cedar cloth and there were few trees around the bowl at that time, it being closer to the beach than it is now. I heard these words to begin the story:

"When we gaze into this bowl we are drawn into the sky, flying in brotherhood with the World to find the reasons for our tribe's misfortune, or how we can call the whales back to our beach after the cold. It is our gateway, the opening between these worlds into which we can fly. We dive into the sky from this bowl edge. We are the guardians of this gateway, and we guide and protect the shaman during his flight...all worlds flow to one."

The picture changed then to show two youths, young men, coming from the sea in initiation, to add their carvings to the growing number of faces around the bowl. Perhaps an initiation into the shamanic tradition included adding their eyes to those that had already begun to define the bowl's edge. As I watched the youths carving their faces in the bowl on that winter's day so long ago, I heard the spirit speak:

"We have each come in our own turn, to add our mark to the edge of the pool; to be watchers for our land. We have come alone with

Part of Shamans' Pool, Kulleet Bay. (COURTESY OF RAY HILL)

spirit to add our face to the circle. In the beginning the World watched as life took form. Each animal and plant was given for the Spirit of Place...cedar trees and abalone each their own role to fill. The world was birthing itself, and would become aware as life became aware. We are to be reminders of the witness. We sit in council watching the World unfold, as our people watch the seasons change. And so we add our eyes to the eyes of the World."

A hush had fallen over this area of the forest while the reading was taking place. Beth stood at the side of the bowl, gazing at the carvings, her hands at her sides. I walked over to her and as we stood there in the mystical stillness with golden sunlight filtering through the burnished maples, we each expressed our gratitude to the spirit of the bowl.

On our way back to the car, we paused at the edge of the energy field, the veil, that surrounded the site, and had great fun walking back and forth through it, so that Beth could get a clear sense of its edge. We then returned to the car so Beth could tape this reading at the Shamans' Pool in Kulleet Bay.

Dyan Grant-Francis, Victoria, B.C.

Every rock, flower, star, animal and person — everything we know — vibrates with life and has within it unique patterns of energy that can be perceived and felt. The only ingredient necessary to read energy is an open heart and a willingness to listen with an open mind.

One sunny morning I went for a walk on the beach with Marcy Wolters. She told me about the petroglyphs of Quadra Island and showed me a very wonderful rock with a well-known native image known as the "Seawolf." I remember being excited at the prospect of seeing these ancient carvings up close. At first glance, one may not notice them as they look like part of the rock. Then, upon closer examination a wonderful image appears in the stone. We sat with the rock for a long time simply enjoying the beach, the sun and the sea air together. We decided to return at a later date with the express purpose of reading the energy of the rock. Our group consisted of an artist, Jim Leishman, Hilary Stewart, a well-known author of historical Pacific Northwest native traditions and life, Marcy and me. Joy awaited our return.

I have found that I can read the energy of people, animals and objects. Reading the energy of objects is called "psychometry." Any form carries within it the original blueprint of its creation. It also carries the energy of those who have influenced it in any way and usually feelings surface that correspond with the image. The Seawolf rock is about four feet above the ground so it was easy to reach. I began by putting my hands on the rock and opening myself to the feelings and images imbued within the rock's energy field. It is important to know that any object holds the consciousness of the person that influenced it with their thoughts and ideas. So, a petroglyph will hold the consciousness of the person that made the carving: his or her reason for making the picture and the story it was meant to convey.

The story began to come in a lovely flow of energy. I saw the Seawolf looking out over the water when I felt the energy of the whales very strongly and searched for the story the carver was trying to convey. The rock was feeling very sad because of the loss of its real connection between the people, the whales and wolves. The rock went on to unfold the story of how the whales and the wolves are really the same being. They showed me the way they pack and hunt together, how their social structures are similar. I began to understand that the Seawolf is really the whale and wolf in one: one mastering the sea and one mastering the land.

In native tradition the elements and man were always seen as working together for the common good of all. It didn't surprise me to be told that the whales actually held the energy that made it possible for the carver to bring the image of the Seawolf into form on the rock. I felt intense energy in my feet as this awareness came into my consciousness.

I knew there was more. I could feel the energy of the whales urging me on as I entered deeper into the consciousness of the Seawolf. I seemed to move through dimensional frequencies and layers of light as I felt whales beneath me. I wondered out loud how much sand had accumulated over the years on this quiet beach and I knew then that if we looked we would find the whales. As we stepped back it was obvious that the very rock on which the Seawolf was carved had the form of a whale, right down to its eye in exactly the right place.

The four of us found pieces of wood that would clear away the sand from the rock and we began to dig. Behind this big whale rock we found a baby whale nestled up against what I felt to be its mother. The rock told me it was a transformed whale and how happy it was that we had unearthed its story. The whale and the wolf are one being.

With this experience to encourage us, Marcy and I went in search of another petroglyph rock called "The Lovers," at Francisco Point (L5).

This was a very happy rock that told its story with great joy. It was easy to read the energy of this rock because of the uplifting vibrations that were intrinsic to it. The story unfolded about a boy and a girl of high status who were from different villages, brought together by the elders in marriage. I could feel the energy of a great celebration along with the hope that this marriage would mend the rift that had been present between these two villages for so long. It had been an arranged marriage but the village also recognized that there would be real love between these two people. This love would ensure their union.

The Lovers rock has the image of two faces with interlocking arms below. Extending to the left and above these figures is an image reminiscent of the sun. The feeling was that this image may have been made at a different time than the faces but that it was part of the story. The sun blessed this marriage, but it also represented the blessing of a Spirit greater than the sun.

As I lifted my hands from the rock I was filled with the images and feelings of the people who were involved at that time. Also the feelings of the carver entrusted with bringing the energy forth in image form. Again, feelings of gratitude flooded me, gratitude that the story could again be heard and felt in this way.

AlixSandra Parness,
Inner Focus School for Advanced Energy Healing, Seattle

ENDNOTES

Introduction
1. Mitchell, "Archaeology of the Gulf Island Area," *Syesis*, supp.
1, 1971:9
2. Assu, 1989:71
3. White, Howard, 1990:119

Part One
1. White, Ellen, public address, Malaspina College, 1996
2. York, Daly, Arnett, 1996:276
3. *Ibid*:277
4. Carlson, 1976:128
5 Lundy, Doris, personal communication, 1993
6. Dowson, *The Daily Telegraph*, London, Sept. 27, 1996:18
7. Hill, 1975:17
8. Emmons, *American Anthropologist*, Vol. 10, 1908:221
9. Boas, 1916:24
10. Barnett, 1955:89.
11. *Ibid*:90
12. Colfax, personal communication, 1996
13. Bouchard, 1986:164
14. Bouchard and Kennedy, 1983:105-106
15. Williams, Judith, personal communication, 1997
16. Heizer, 1953:34
17. Beal, 1994:19
18. *Ibid*:19
18. Tait, 1900:320.
20. Lundy 1977:57
21. Heizer 1953:34.
22. Driver in Heizer, 1953:35
23. White, Ellen, public address, Malaspina College, 1996
24. Duff, 1967:19
25. Shadbolt, 1986:26
26. Davidson, 1993:86

Part Two
1. Assu 1989:31
2. Meade, 1971:42

107

SOURCES

Abbott, Don, ed. *The World is as Sharp as a Knife.* Anthology in Honour of Wilson Duff. British Columbia Provincial Museum, Victoria, 1981

Assu, Harry with Joy Inglis. *Assu of Cape Mudge, Recollections of a Coastal Indian Chief.* University of British Columbia Press, Vancouver, 1989

Barnett, Homer. *The Coast Salish Indians of British Columbia.* University of Oregon Press, Eugene, 1955

Beal, John. "Shaman's Drum," reprinted from *The Joy Gazette,* 1994

Bentley, Mary and Ted. *Gabriola: Petroglyph Island.* Sono Nis Press, Victoria, 1981

Berodzky, Anne, Rose Danesewich and Nick Johnson, eds. *Stones, Bones and Skin, Ritual and Shamanic Art.* The Society for Art Publications, Toronto, 1977

Boas, Franz. *Bella Bella Tales.* American Folklore Society, G.E. Stechert, New York, 1932. Reprinted, Kraus Reprint Co., 1973

Boas, Franz and George Hunt. "Kwakiutl Texts," *Jesup North Pacific Expedition.* Memoir of the American Museum of Natural History, Vol. 10, 1906

Bouchard, Randy and Dorothy Kennedy. *Sliammon Life, Sliammon Land.* TalonBooks, Vancouver, 1983

Carlson, Roy R. "The North Pacific to 1600," *Proceedings of the Great Ocean Conferences.* North Pacific Study Center. Oregon Historical Society, 1991

Carlson, Roy R. "Content and Chronology of Northwest Coast (North America) Rock Art." Reprinted from *Time and Space.* Second AURA Congress, Cairns, J. Steinberg and Alan Watchman, eds 1992

Carlson, Roy R., ed. *Indian Art Traditions of the Northwest Coast.* Department of Archaeology, Simon Fraser University, Vancouver, 1976

Corner, John. *Petroglyphs in the Interior of British Columbia,* Wayside Press, Vernon, 1968

Curtis, Edward. "The Kwakiutl," *The North American Indian.* Vol.10. Plimpton Press, Nordwood, 1915

Davidson, Robert. *Eagle of the Dawn.* Ean M. Thom, Ed., Douglas & McIntyre, Vancouver, 1993

108

Dowson, T.A and Lewis Williams. "The Context of Southern San Art," *Current Anthropology*, Vol.29, No.2, 1988

Duff, Wilson. *Arts of the Raven. Masterworks of the Northwest Coast Indian.* The Vancouver Art Gallery, Vancouver, 1967

Duff, Wilson. *Images Stone b.c. Thirty Centuries of Northwest Coast Indian Sculpture.* Hancock House, Saanichton, 1975

Eliade, Mercea. *Shamanism. Archaic Techniques of Ecstasy.* Princeton University Press, Princeton, 1964

Emmons, George T. "Petroglyphs in Southeastern Alaska," *American Anthropologist.* Vol.10, No.2, 1908.

Gunther, Erna. "A Further Analysis of the First Salmon Ceremony," University of Washington Publications in Anthropology, No.5, Vol.2, 1925

Harris, Cole. "Voices of Disaster: Smallpox Around the Strait of Georgia in 1782," *Out of the Background. Readings on Canadian Native History*, Second Edition, Coates and Fisher, eds. Copp Clarke Ltd., Toronto, 1996

Heizer, Robert F. "Sacred Rain Rocks of Northern California," University of California Archaeological Survey No.20, 1953

Hill, Beth and Ray. *Indian Petroglyphs of the Pacific Northwest.* Hancock House, Saanichton, 1974

Hill, Beth. *Guide to Indian Rock Carvings of the Pacific Northwest.* Hancock House, Saanichton, 1975

Hill, Beth. *Bedrock and Boulder Bowls.* Hancock House, Saanichton, 1975

Hill, Beth. *Seven-Knot Summers.* Horsdal & Schubart, Victoria, 1994

Hill, Beth. *Moonrakers.* Horsdal & Schubart, Victoria, 1997

Katz-La Haigue, Vaniana. "Shamanic Content in the Art of Clayoquot Artist, Joe David." Dissertation, Department of Anthropology, University of British Columbia, 1983

Leland, Donald and Donald Mitchell. "Some correlates of local group ranking amongst Southern Kwakiulth," *Syesis*, Vol. 14, No.4, 1975

Lundy, Doris. "Rock Art of the Northwest Coast." Unpublished MA thesis, Department of Archaeology, Simon Fraser University, Vancouver, 1974

Lundy, Doris. "The Conventionalized Rock Art Style," in *Indian Art Traditions of the Northwest Coast*, Roy Carlson, ed. Simon Fraser University, Vancouver, 1976

Lundy, Doris. "The Petroglyphs of the British Columbia Interior," CRARA, 77. Papers from the Fourth Biennial Conference of the Canadian Rock Art Research Association, Doris Lundy, ed. Heritage Record 8, British Columbia Provincial Museum, Victoria, 1979
MacDonald, George. "Prehistoric Art of the Northwest Coast," in *Indian Art Traditions of the Northwest Coast,* Roy Carlson, ed. Simon Fraser University, Vancouver, 1976
MacDonald, George. *The Shamans' Doorway.* Video. National Museum of Canada, Ottawa, 1976
MacDonald, George. "Cosmic Equations in Northwest Coast Indian Art," in *The World is as Sharp as a Knife,* Don Abbott, ed. British Columbia Provincial Museum, Victoria, 1981
McMaster, Gerald and Lee Anne Martin, eds. *Indigena.* Canadian Museum of Civilization, Hull, 1992
McMurdo, Ann. "Excavation of a petroglyph site on Protection Island, British Columbia," CRARA 77. Papers from the Fourth Biennial Conference of the Canadian Rock Art Research Association, Doris Lundy, ed. Heritage Record 8, British Columbia Provincial Museum, Victoria, 1979
MacNair, Peter, Alan Hoover and Kent Neary. *The Legacy: Continuing Traditions of Canadian Northwest Coast Indian Art.* British Columbia Provincial Museum, Victoria, 1980
Meade, Edward. *Indian Rock Carvings of the Pacific Northwest.* Gray's Publishing, Sidney, 1971
Newton, Norman. "On Survivals of Ancient Astronomical Ideas Among the Peoples of the Northwest Coast," *B.C. Studies.* University of British Columbia, Vancouver, 1975
Okladnikov, Alexie. *Introduction to the Art of the Amur, Ancient Art of the Russian Far East.* Harry M. Abrams Inc., New York City, 1981
Skinner, Mark. *Analysis of Human Skeletal Remains. Site: Cape Mudge Village, Quadra Island, B.C., (EaSh3).* Report to Heritage Conservation Branch, Government of British Columbia, 1986
Stewart, Hilary. *Looking at Indian Art of the Northwest Coast.* Douglas & McIntyre, Vancouver, 1979
Tait, James. "The Thompson Indians of British Columbia," *Jesup North Pacific Expedition,* Memoir of the American Museum of Natural History, Vol 2, 1900
Vancouver, George. *A Voyage of Discovery to the North Pacific Ocean and Round the World, 1791-1795.* Hakluyt Society, London, 1984

Walker, D, and G. Dixon Hepplewhite. "Night Light Petroglyph Photography — a Photographic Technique," CRARA, 77. Papers from the Fourth Biennial Conference of the Canadian Rock Art Research Association, Doris Lundy, ed. Heritage Record 8, British Columbia Provincial Museum, Victoria, 1979

Watson, Scott. "Whose Nation?" *Canadian Art,* Spring, 1993

White Howard. *Writing in the Rain*, Harbour Publishing, Madeira Park, B.C., 1990

Williams, Judith. *High Slack*. New Star Books Ltd., Vancouver, 1996

Williams, Lewis. "The Economic and Social Context of Southern San Rock Art," *Current Anthropology*, August, 1982

York, Annie, Richard Daly and Chris Arnett. *They Write Their Dreams on the Rocks Forever: Rock Writings in the Stein River Valley.* TalonBooks, Vancouver, 1993